# FINANCE FOR NON-FINANCE MANAGERS

Eric Smith

THE BUSINESS LIBRARY

The Business Library
is an imprint of

Information Australia
A.C.N. 006 042 173
45 Flinders Lane
Melbourne VIC 3000
Telephone: (03) 654 2800
Fax: (03) 650 5261

ISBN 1 86350 088 X
Copyright © 1993 by Eric Smith

This is a completely updated edition of The Bottom Line, first published by Penguin Books Australia, 1989.

All rights reserved. This publication is copyright and may not be resold or reproduced in any manner (except excerpts thereof for bona fide study purposes in accordance with the Copyright Act) without the prior consent of the Publisher.

Every effort has been made to ensure that this book is free from error or omissions. However, the Publisher, the Editor, or their respective employees or agents, shall not accept responsibility for injury, loss or damage occasioned to any person acting or refraining from action as a result of material in this book whether or not such injury, loss or damage is in any way due to any negligent act or omission, breach of duty or default on the part of the Publisher, the Editor, or their respective employees or agents.

The National Library of Australia
Cataloguing-in-Publication entry

Smith, Eric (Eric Stephen).
 [Bottom line]. Finance for non-finance managers.

 Bibliography.
 ISBN 1 86350 088 X.

 1. Accounting. 2. Financial statements. I. Title.
 II. Title: Bottom line.

657

Cover design by Optima Design
Printed in Australia by Australian Print Group

## Acknowledgements

Sources of extracts quoted in the text are as follows:

p.3 John Singleton, Rip Van Australia, Cassell, Melbourne, 1977, p. 159; p. 120: W.S. Gilbert, Ruddigore; p. 190 Robert Frost, 'The Hardship of Accounting,' Ten Mills: A Further Range, Jonathan Cape, London, 1936, Estate of Robert Frost, reprinted with permission; pp. 196, 200: Peter Clyne, Outlaw Among Lawyers, Cassell, Melbourne, 1981, p. 111; p. 234, Jack Argenti Systematic Corporate Planning Nelson, Walton-on-Thames, 1974, p. 43.

# Foreword

A company had engaged me to give some financial literacy to a small group of bright young graduates whom they hoped would be the future top management. I had put folders of course notes out for each participant with the heading 'Executive Training Course'. The first one to look at it remarked, 'Jeez, executive training, I must be in the wrong place.'

The word 'executive' is often used very loosely. Some companies have 'junior executives' who collect trolleys from the carpark. So perhaps we could safely use the term to describe anyone who has any management duties or any pretensions towards management. If that is you, whether you work for a large firm, a small firm or yourself, and you have difficulty in understanding what the accountants are up to, this book is for you.

You will find this book more entertaining than 'Chances', more informative than 'Sixty Minutes' and unlike either of them it is tax-deductible.

Eric Smith

# About the Author

Eric Smith grew up in Korumburra, Victoria, with a burning ambition to become a journalist. However, the only way he could afford to go to the university was to sell himself into bondage with the Education Department as a teacher of commercial subjects. Unraveling the mysteries of accounting created a major crisis in his life and he has deep empathy with others forced to develop financial skills against their better instincts.

After leaving the Education Department Eric worked as an accountant and financial manager, a tutor and lecturer in accounting, and a management consultant, before running his own business for six years. In 1982 he returned to tertiary education as a junior tutor at Chisholm Institute of Technology and is now the Principal Lecturer in the School of Accounting and Finance at Deakin University, Melbourne.

Eric Smith is a consultant to many of Australia's leading companies, and is also a prolific writer of short stories and a prize-winning landscape painter.

# Contents

1. **Accounting and the Executive** .............. 1
   - The Assumptions under which Accountants Work .................... 2
   - The Assumptions under which Other Managers Work ..................... 3

2. **Basic Jargon: The Balance Sheet** ............ 8
   - The Accounting Entity ................ 9
   - Assets ............................... 9
   - Liabilities ...........................10
   - The Balance Sheet ...................11
   - Valuing Assets ......................11
   - The Accountant's Meaning of Depreciation .......................13
   - Valuation of Trading Stock ...........14
   - Owners' Equity in a Company - Shareholders' Funds ..................14
   - The Accounting Cycle ................16
   - How Transactions Are Processed through the System ..................18
   - The Rules of Debit and Credit .........21

3. **More Basic Jargon: The Profit and Loss Statement** ...............................26
   - The Profit and Loss Statement .........26
   - The Balance Sheet ...................28
   - The Funds Statement .................31

4. **Financing the Business** .....................34
   - Equity Finance and Debt Finance .......34
   - The Risk-Free Rate ..................35

- The Premium for Risk .................35
- The Opportunity Rate ................36
- Aversion to Risk ....................36
- The Golden Rule of Finance ..........37
- Effects of Tax Deductibility of Interest Payments ...........................37
- Gearing of Company Finance ..........38
- Security of Lenders and Shareholders ....39
- Sources of Short-Term Finance ..........39
- Discounts for Prompt Payment ..........41
- Sources of Long-Term Finance ..........42
- Calculating the Company's Cost of Capital ..............................44
- The Cost of Debt Capital ...............44
- The Cost of Equity Capital .............44

5. **Planning to Make Profits** .....................49
   - Sales Planning ........................49
   - Sales Forecasting......................49
   - Calculating a Target Profit ..............52
   - Fixed and Variable Costs ...............53
   - The Contribution Margin ...............54
   - The Break-Even Point ..................55

6. **Into the Heart of Break-Even Analysis** .........57
   - The Contribution Margin Ratio .........57
   - Break-even Analysis for Retailers ........58
   - The Margin of Safety .................59
   - Operating Leverage ...................60
   - Using Contribution Margin as a Basis for Sales Commissions ...................61
   - Using Contribution Margin to Optimise the Sales Mix .......................61
   - Break-Even Analysis and Proposed New Products ...........................62

- The Learning Curve Effect ............ 63

7. **Mapping the Road to Success: Budgeting** ...... 66
    - Long-Term Planning ................... 67
    - Intermediate-Term Planning ........... 69
    - Annual Budgets ....................... 71
    - The Master Budget .................... 72
    - The Sales Budget ..................... 74
    - The Production Budget ................ 75
    - The Direct Materials Budget .......... 76
    - The Direct Labour Budget ............. 77
    - The Manufacturing Overheads Budget ... 78
    - The Finished Goods Inventory Budget ... 79
    - The Selling and Administrative Expenses Budget ............................. 80
    - The Cash Budget ...................... 81
    - The Budgeted Financial Statements ...... 84
    - The Budgeted Balance Sheet and Budgeted Funds Statement ............. 84
    - Zero Base Budgeting .................. 86
    - The Budget as a Control Mechanism ..... 87
    - Management by Exception ............. 87
    - Responsibility Accounting ............ 88
    - Performance Reports .................. 88
    - Flexible Budgets ..................... 90

8. **Working Capital Management** ................ 92
    - Working Capital ...................... 92
    - Ensuring the Business Has the Right Composition of Assets ................. 93
    - Labour as an Asset ................... 93
    - Managing Cash as an Asset ............ 95
    - Managing Debtors .................... 95
    - Managing Stocks ..................... 96
    - Managing Plant and Equipment ......... 97

- Owning the Right Quantity of Assets ..... 97
- The Operating Cycle ................... 98
- The Three Phases of the Operating Cycle ................................. 99
- The Stock Turn or Stock Turnover Rate ................................. 100
- Debtors Turnover Rate ............... 102

## 9. Inventory Control ........................... 107
- The Golden Rule of Inventory Planning ............................. 108
- Factors to Consider in Planning Inventories .......................... 109
- The ABC Method of Inventory Control ............................... 110
- Lead Time and Safety Stocks ........... 111
- Economic Order Quantity .............. 114
- Economic Production Run .............. 117
- Just-in-Time Inventory Management ..... 118

## 10. Planning Capital Expenditure ................ 121
- Capital Budgeting .................... 122
- The Payback Method .................. 123
- The Accounting Rate of Return ......... 125
- Discounted Cash Flow Methods (DCF) ............................... 126
- The Net Present Value Method ......... 134
- The Internal Rate of Return Method ..... 135
- Cost/Benefit Ratio .................... 137
- Time-Adjusted Payback ................ 138
- Capital Rationing .................... 139

## 11. Controlling Expenses ....................... 142
- Responsibility Centres ................ 143
- Cost Centres ......................... 143

- Revenue Centres .................... 144
- Profit Centres ...................... 144
- Investment Centres ................. 144
- Performance Reports ............... 145
- Engineered Expenses ............... 148
- Managed Expenses .................. 149
- Standard Costing Systems .......... 149
- Material Price Variance and Material Usage Variance ..................... 154

## 12. Revenue Centres: Little Goldmines or ...? ..... 164
- Responsibilities of the Revenue Centre Manager ........................... 164
- The Problem of Maintaining Sales Revenue ........................... 167
- Sales Price Variance ................ 170
- The Sales Volume Variance ......... 171
- The Contribution Margin Mix Variance ........................... 172
- Importance of Market Share ........ 173
- The Sales Manager and Debtors Turnover and Stock Turn ........... 174
- The Backlog of Orders Report ...... 175
- Advertising Expenditure ............ 175
- Sales Representatives' Performance Reports ........................... 175
- Customer Reports .................. 177
- Control of Travel and Entertainment Costs ............................. 177

## 13. Profit Centres and Investment Centres ........ 179
- Profit Centres ...................... 179
- Setting Objectives for Profit Centres ..... 180
- Transfer Pricing Between Divisions ...... 184
- The Revenue Control Problem ........ 188
- Investment Centres ................. 191

- Measuring Performance in an Investment Centre .............................. 192
- Measuring Return on Investment (ROI) .................................... 192
- Residual Income ...................... 193

## 14. Taxes and More Taxes ...................... 196
- PAYE Income Tax .................... 197
- Provisional Income Tax ............... 199
- Prescribed Payments Scheme .......... 200
- Company Income Tax .................. 202
- The Dividend Imputation System ....... 203
- Entertainment Expenses are not Usually Tax Deductible ...................... 204
- Capital Gains Tax .................... 206
- Fringe Benefits Tax (FBT) ............. 209
- Sales Tax ........................... 211
- Payroll Tax ......................... 212
- Stamp Duty ......................... 212
- Excise Duty ........................ 213
- Local Government Taxes .............. 213

## 15. Service Industries ........................ 215
- The Special Characteristics of Service Industries ........................... 216
- Performance Measurement in Service Industries ........................... 219
- Everybody is a Marketer in a Service Industry ............................ 221
- Pricing of Services .................... 222
- Use of Management Accounting Techniques .......................... 223
- Service Firms and Break-Even Analysis ............................ 223
- Other Measures of Performance ......... 224
- Profitability Analysis of Services ........ 225

## 16. Out-Guessing the Competition: Planning and Strategy ... 228
- The Need to Plan ... 229
- Corporate Planning ... 229
- What Is in the Corporate Plan? ... 230
- Who Does the Planning? ... 231
- Corporate Objectives ... 232
- The Position Audit ... 234
- Company-Based Strategies ... 236
- Customer-Based Strategies ... 237
- Competitor-Based Strategies ... 239
- Using Financial Information as a Competitive Tool ... 240

# 1

## Accounting and the Executive

My colleague was less than impressed.

'So what you mean is that you're going to write a book on finance that even people like marketers and engineers could understand.'

'Something like that.'

'What, a sort of "John and Betty go to the Stock Exchange"?'

'Well not exactly.'

'It can't be done you know. Marketing people have left-side brains, we have right-side brains. We can't write and they can't understand.'

This is an over-simplification of the situation, but the fact is that too often there is little common ground between accountants and other executives. However, for business to operate at its optimum level of efficiency, accountants must understand the roles of other executive staff, and every decision-maker must have a good grasp of finance. For several years now I have run a course called 'Financial Control for Non-finance Executives' and in the newspaper advertisement for the course we use the words: **If you're an executive aiming for the top, you need to know all about the bottom line.** Ain't it the truth!

## The Assumptions under which Accountants Work

Before we get too heavily into financial matters it is best to find out the assumptions under which accountants and other types of managers operate. Accountants used to assume that the aim of business was to maximise profits. However, these days most of us have modified the aim of business to 'maximisation of shareholder wealth'.

This is not quite the same thing. It presumes a continuing long-term commitment to wealth generation even at the cost of not maximising profits in the short run. Therefore, in reviewing the financial situation, the accountant may consider certain short-term gains as not being in the longer-term interests of the business. If businesses always aimed to maximise short-term profits, they would not spend money on staff development or sponsor sport.

The accountant's task is more specifically to protect the financial interests of the shareholders by looking after the assets; and to provide financial information that can be used in making business decisions. The latter requires the careful recording and reporting of financial information.

It is sometimes said that the accountant only provides the information for decision-making and that the decisions are made by others acting on that information. You and I both know that this is not entirely true. Many accountants make financial decisions that affect, infuriate, even destroy, their non-accounting colleagues. It is not surprising that the image of the accountant is of a reserved conservative plotter, manipulating the business behind the scenes, fiddling the finances while everybody else burns.

One major problem is that accountants do not have the same point of view as the people they work with. Their assumptions are different. Well what are the assumptions that other managers are working from?

## The Assumptions under which Other Managers Work

John Singleton once wrote:

> Marketing is a nonsense term invented by people who are trying to hide the fact that either: (1) they are salesmen who would rather be school teachers, or (2) they are salesmen who are so ineffectual and stupid that they might as well be school teachers.

He should know - marketing has made him a millionaire - but perhaps he was a little tongue in cheek.

Modern concepts of marketing include all parts of the process of making a sale. The marketing process starts with the concept of the product, its design and its production, and carries through to promotion, distribution and sale of the product. However, the critical point in the process is selling. An old adage says: 'Nothing happens until somebody sells something.' You can have a beautifully organised business, with the ultimate in financial geniuses and a string of brilliant MBAs running things, but if there are no sales the whole thing goes down the gurgler.

It is no accident that the accountant starts the calculation of profit with the sales figure. The marketer is dedicated to selling at whatever cost, and because this requires interaction with customers, marketers are often seen by accountants as extroverted, gregarious and uncaring about such little things as record-keeping and expense control.

As manufacturing becomes more sophisticated, firms recruit more engineering graduates for executive positions. This makes a lot of sense because they are generally intelligent and diligent. In most cases, however, they have received no business training in their courses and this leaves them under-prepared for the trauma of management. They are faced with many problems and fundamental misunderstandings in their dealings with accountants. These problems include:

- The jargon barrier. Accountants, like other professionals, surround themselves with a language which means little to the uninitiated.

- Lack of certainty. Most financial decisions are made without any certainty of result. Engineers are used to situations where, if a certain course of action is taken, the result is inevitable. Financial people may treat an outcome as being very probable, but there is no certainty.

- The single solution myth. Precision is part of the accountant's image. A mass of information is processed and a single solution emerges; for instance, the net profit for the year. There is no indication that it contains many estimates and arbitrary figures, such as rates of depreciation, capital profits, revaluation of assets and method of stock valuation. The choice of a different figure in any of these areas could produce quite a different profit result. In fact, with very few variable numbers, the profit calculated could be any one of a million different figures. Yet accountants always try to cling to single solutions, to the profit figure. Problems arise because accountants themselves know that the single solution is a myth and they compensate for it, but others are left to cling to the single figure without that understanding.

Managers from other backgrounds such as purchasing, administration, secretarial functions, personnel and production all have similar problems in dealing with accountants. These problems are often serious enough to hinder their careers or frustrate them into looking for another position.

One cause of conflict between accountants and other managers is that the starting point is different. Marketing, for example, starts with thinking about the situation in an external market. Accounting starts with the analysis of internal costs and financial figures. If an accountant was asked to assess a market, the starting point would probably be previous figures for the existing market. The marketer must take a much broader approach, including the nature of customers and competitors and economic conditions.

Engineers have a similar problem. When an engineer looks at a production problem, it is in terms of engineered solutions, not the solution that costs less but compromises quality or product life. The accountant is likely to see the problem as purely a matter of the cheapest way out. A personnel officer may see the solution to a lack of qualified staff as a matter of staff development at company cost. The accountant may see a more cost-effective solution in changing to a new method of production. The purchasing officer may know that a higher price must be paid for a product to keep a source of supply viable. The accountant may see it as over-paying. With this sort of fundamental conflict, it is no wonder that misunderstandings and tensions occur.

- Some of the basic assumptions of accounting do not fit other managers. Accounting's most basic assumption is that revenue and expense in a period can be matched together to provide a profit figure for that period. Marketers and others may find the division of time into accounting periods too restrictive. In their view, profitability stems from the firm's position within various market segments and the longer-term surpluses created. Engineers may see the future benefits of the learning curve. Financial control of the marketing function should take into consideration the patterns of sales revenue and competition that do not necessarily coincide with the ends of accounting periods.

To make matters worse, many accountants are unfamiliar with the concept of the product life cycle and the need to allow for growth and decay periods in that life cycle. They are also unaware of the value of market share over the product life, the need to maintain it, and the serious costs in losing market share. There is no recognition of market share at all in accounting figures. Engineers become frustrated that accountants cannot see the longer-term implications of not completing scheduled maintenance. Too great an attachment to cost cutting can be counter-productive.

- The costing unit used by accountants may not be appropriate to anybody else. Products are usually costed according to some characteristic selected in the production process. The criterion is usually some standard input. For example, white cotton shirts may be costed on a per unit basis. Once this basis is selected, all financial analysis will be made according to it. However, the profitability of the product may arise out of the segments in which it is sold. White cotton shirts sold through menswear stores may be potentially more profitable than those sold through supermarket chains. Those sold on credit may be more profitable than those sold for cash. However, accounting in its usual form seldom, if ever, allows for separate costing or separate profit calculations according to market segment (although perhaps it should). Even where accountants calculate profits for segments of the business, these will rarely coincide with market segments. Engineers may prefer their calculations to be made according to production runs rather than lumping the production from several runs in together.

These are just a few samples of fundamental problems that arise in the dealings between accountants, and managers from other discipline backgrounds. What can be done about this situation of conflict? The answer, in the short term, is **very little**. However, in the longer term, whether you are an engineer, purchaser, marketer or whatever, you must work out your information needs and communicate them to the accounting staff. Accountants are only employed because they carry out a useful function. That is, they supply financial information to others for decision-making purposes. If you did not need their information the firm would not need them. Remember that.

It is essential that you understand the way in which the accounting system operates and the many ways in which it can help you. This book will not make you into an accountant; however, it will make you familiar with financial techniques, reports and practices. It will give you sufficient financial knowledge to do better than survive.

# 2

# Basic Jargon: The Balance Sheet

Harry made my day.

I was running an executive training course for a large manufacturing company and Harry was a bright young plant manager who for two days had wrestled with the mysteries of finance. About eleven o'clock on the third day Harry took a telephone call from the firm's financial accountant. The accountant began to attack Harry about the return on investment achieved by his plant.

'But you have to remember,' Harry replied, 'those assets are valued at historical cost and they don't reflect the true rate of return. Anyway you have allocated costs to the plant which are not controllable by me. I suggest that we get together and discuss a more realistic calculation base.' There was a stunned silence for about twenty seconds.

'Well,' answered a subdued voice, 'er ... Let's do that.' Then another silence. 'Tell me, Harry, where the hell did you get that from? What else have they told you?' Harry came back glowing with satisfaction.

The concepts in finance and accounting are easy to understand. As in many other areas of knowledge, the main problem is getting through the jargon barrier. I once saw a little poem at the start of an economics book, which could be used to describe financial matters. It was the recipe for academic success:

> When all the roads to fame are barred,
> Take something easy, and make it hard.

A full understanding of the terms used will always make it easier to understand the whole picture.

## The Accounting Entity

In accounting we assume that the affairs of any business are always separated from the private affairs of the owner. This is the case, even if the business does not exist as a separate legal entity, as in a sole proprietorship or a partnership. It is the business that we are accounting for. An 'entity' is something with a separate existence. A business is an accounting entity and anything that happens financially in the business must be seen from the point of view of that entity, not of its owners. If the owners put in capital to get the business started, then the business owes that amount to the owners. Any profits made by the business are also owing to those owners. Owner's equity (or proprietorship) is the name given to this capital and accumulated profits. In a company it will be called shareholders' funds.

## Assets

Assets are items of value owned by the business, such as land, buildings, investments, cash, stock and plant. In financial statements, assets are usually classified as:

- current assets or
- noncurrent assets.

Current assets are those assets which are either in the form of cash, or are likely to be used up or converted into cash within the next twelve months. Some examples are cash, debtors, stocks and prepaid expenses. They are classified separately because they represent amounts that are relatively easily converted into cash in a crisis.

Non-current assets are assets not likely to be converted into cash within the next twelve months. This will include productive assets (sometimes called fixed assets) like plant, buildings, land, machinery and delivery vehicles; intangible assets like goodwill and patent rights; long-term investments in shares and other securities; and other non-current items like long-term loans to employees.

## Liabilities

Liabilities are the amounts owed by the business to people or businesses other than the owners. These liabilities can be classified in the same way as assets, into:

- current liabilities; and
- long term (or deferred) liabilities.

Current liabilities are those which must be paid within the next twelve months. Some examples would be creditors, taxes owing and expenses still owing at the end of an accounting period.

Long-term liabilities (or deferred liabilities) do not have to be paid within the next twelve months. Examples would be long service leave owing in the future for years of service already completed and long-term loans of various kinds. Again, it is necessary to classify the liabilities into current and long-term because the current liabilities could cause short-term financial problems. As we shall see, the comparison of current assets with current liabilities gives us some indication of the short-term financial stability of the business.

Since all the assets held by the business are financed by the owners or by borrowings from others, at all times:

>Assets = Liabilities + Owners' Equity
>or
>Assets = Equities

This relationship, which is the basis of all accounting, is called the accounting equation.

## The Balance Sheet

The balance sheet is an accounting statement which is based on the accounting equation. The Americans call it the Statement of Financial Position. It shows the assets owned by the business, its liabilities and owners' equity. There are many different ways in which the balance sheet may be presented but a simple example is given in Figure 2.1.

**Figure 2.1**
**SAM'S GARDENING SERVICE**
**Balance Sheet as at 30 June 19--**

| ASSETS | $ | EQUITIES | | $ |
|---|---|---|---|---|
| *Current assets* | | *Current liabilities* | | |
| Cash | 400 | Creditors | | 700 |
| Debtors | 1 600 | Wages owing | | 400 |
| Stock of supplies | 700 | | | |
| | | *Owners' equity* | | |
| *Non-current assets* | | Capital | $4 000 | |
| Equipment | 3 200 | Profit | 800 | 4 800 |
| TOTAL ASSETS | $5 900 | TOTAL EQUITIES | | $5 900 |

The $5,900 worth of assets owned by Sam's Gardening Service is financed mainly by Sam's capital and profits. The few liabilities of the business could easily be met out of current assets. If Sam closed up business at this date and the equipment could be sold at the value shown, the debts could be paid and Sam would receive $4,800, the amount of owners' equity. However, if Sam wanted to take out half of his capital on this date, there would be a problem because there is only $400 in cash and $1,100 is owing to other people. Sam could not even take out all of his profit without waiting for some of the debtors to pay.

## Valuing Assets

Financial information is useful only when it is expressed in dollar amounts. Liabilities are valued at the amount owing, but valuing assets is not so simple. Consider as an example a small piece of production plant. It is five years old but should last another five years. It originally cost $40,000. It could be removed and resold for a net sum of $5,000. During the next five years it will produce $60,000 worth of goods. It would cost $70,000 to replace with a similar model.

The possible valuations that could be used are:

(a) its original cost of $40,000;

(b) its original cost, halved to recognise the fact that half of its life has been used up, that is $20,000;

(c) its market value of $5000;

(d) the $60,000 it can earn over the rest of its life;

(e) its $70,000 replacement cost.

All of these possible bases of valuation have something in their favour. However:

(a) does not take into account the fact that the plant's life has been half used up;

(c) may not be accurate as it is only an estimate;

(d) is also only an estimate and much of that production is so far into the future that the dollars earned may have lost value; and

(e) ignores the fact that technology changes. The replacement machine is likely to be quite different, with higher capacity and reduced running costs.

Although alternative (b) is not ideal at least it shows the amount originally paid and allows for expiry of some of the value through use. So in the valuation of fixed assets, accountants usually adopt the rule of using the original cost of the asset adjusted for the part of its life that has been used up. This part of the asset's life that has been used up is referred to as depreciation.

## The Accountant's Meaning of Depreciation

When we used the word 'depreciation' in everyday life, we use it to mean loss of market value. We may say that a car has depreciated because a new model has come on to the market or because it has been wrapped around a lamp post. This is not what accountants mean by depreciation. In accounting, depreciation simply means the part of the asset's lifetime that has expired.

Consider again that piece of plant which is half-way through its ten-year life and cost $40,000. The purpose of depreciation is to spread the cost of the asset across its lifetime. If the plant cost $40,000 and lasts ten years then we can allocate part of its cost as an expense in each of those years rather than charge the whole amount against the expenses of the year in which it was purchased. This will not change the fact that the full amount must be paid for the plant at the time of purchase. It is simply a convenient way of spreading costs in calculating profit. The amount of depreciation shown on the piece of plant in each year would be:

$$\frac{\$40\,000 \text{ cost}}{10 \text{ years of life}} = \$4000 \text{ per annum}$$

The value of this piece of plant in the balance sheet, at the end of the first year, would be shown as:

| | | |
|---|---|---|
| Plant (at cost) | $40 000 | |
| Less: accumulated depreciation | $4000 | $36 000 |

The net value of $36,000 is called its book value. It will probably bear no relationship at all to the value for which it could be sold at that time. As more depreciation is written off each year the amount of accumulated depreciation will grow so that the book value becomes smaller. After five years the balance sheet would show:

|  |  |  |
|---|---|---|
| Plant (at cost) | $40 000 | |
| Less: accumulated depreciation | $20 000 | $20 000 |

Since all fixed assets are usually shown in the balance sheet on this basis and not at their market value, it is quite clear that the value shown for assets in the balance sheet is likely to be very different from their market value.

**The balance sheet is not intended to be used as a statement of the current values of the assets.** Even where the asset is not depreciated, as with land for instance, it may be shown at its cost price of several years earlier or at an assessment of its value by the directors.

### Valuation of Trading Stock

Trading stock is usually shown at the 'lower of cost or net realisable value', not at its selling price. This means that normally stock is valued at cost. However, if there is a reason to believe that its market value is less than cost, it will be valued at that lower value, less the costs involved in selling it. You will appreciate that this is a very conservative basis on which to value stock.

**So the total value of assets in the balance sheet is likely to be nothing like their true market value.** There is nothing dishonest about this. Re-valuing the assets every time their market value changes would be just as confusing and would be largely done according to estimates and guesswork. However, you should remember to never treat a balance sheet as a list of values at which assets could be sold. If a company balance sheet shows total assets at $5 million, it means that we can be sure of only one thing about their market value. That is, that they are not worth $5 million.

### Owners' Equity in a Company - Shareholders' Funds

A company is owned by its shareholders. So the owner's equity in a company consists of the share capital and reserves, sometimes called shareholders' funds. Share capital is the face value of shares issued by the company. When the company is registered, it is authorised to issue a certain number of shares of a certain value. For instance, it may be registered to issue 4 million shares of 50 cents each. In this case its **authorised or registered capital** is $2 million.

Only in exceptional cases would these shares all be issued immediately. The promoters of the company may decide to issue only half of them so that the **issued capital** would be $1 million. If the subscribers who buy them pay the full face value immediately, the **paid up capital** is also $1 million.

Shareholders receive returns on their shares in the form of **dividends**. Dividends are declared at so many cents per share. They are usually paid in two parts; an interim dividend part of the way through the year; and a final dividend after the end of the financial year. Usually companies distribute only part of the profits as dividends to the shareholders. The remainder is kept by the company to assist in expansion.

**Retained earnings or undistributed profits** represent profits that have not been paid out as dividends. This amount is a **reserve**. Reserves are commonly of two major kinds: **revenue reserves** and **capital reserves**.

Revenue reserves arise from undistributed profits; these may be given a variety of names including general reserve, retained earnings, dividend equalisation reserve, and profit and loss appropriation.

Capital reserves arise out of capital profits. The two most common of these are the **asset revaluation reserve**, which is created when land or buildings increase in value; and **share premium reserve**, which is created if a company manages to issue shares at more than their face value.

For example, assume the company we mentioned earlier was successful in its first year of operations and decided to issue another million of its shares to the public. If the company is successful, its 50 cent face value shares may be selling on the Stock Exchange at $2 because the trading price for shares depends on supply and demand. It would be silly for the company to issue its new shares for only 50 cents each, because it would be swamped by speculators buying the shares and selling them at an immediate profit. So the company may decide to issue the 50 cent shares at a $1.20 premium per share. Buyers still get a good deal at $1.70 per share and the company picks up all of those extra $1.20s. This would create a share premium reserve of $1.2 million which the company can use for expansion. However, just because a company has this reserve it does not mean that somewhere it is keeping a big bag of cash. The funds from the reserve will be tied up in the various assets of the company. To get cash those assets may have to be liquidated.

## The Accounting Cycle

Accounting is a systematic method of dealing with financial information. The method which we use today was invented in the fifteenth century in the Italian merchant state of Genoa. It relies on the fact that every transaction has at least two effects on the accounting equation. For this reason, it is called double-entry accounting. Broadly speaking, the movement of information through the accounting system has the following phases.

1   **Source documents.** These are the pieces of original evidence that a transaction has taken place. Source documents include invoices for goods purchased, duplicate invoices of goods sold, cheque lists from computer-prepared cheques, cash-register rolls showing money received, credit notes and payments vouchers. In short, all of those bits and pieces of paper that people sometimes throw in a drawer and forget. These documents are the raw material of accounting and if they are not fed into the system properly, all of the accounting reports will be wrong. It's no wonder that accountants become paranoid about little bits of paper.

2   **Journals.** Journal is an old French word which means 'day book'. Journals are used to record the details from the source documents. They act as summaries of the transactions, grouping together those transactions which are similar in nature. Most firms have special journals where there are a lot of similar transactions. The usual journals are:

**Cash payments journal** for all transactions where money is paid out.

**Cash receipts journal** for all transactions where money is received.

**Sales journal** for all credit sales of stock.

**Purchases journal** for all credit purchases of stock.

**Sales returns and allowances journal** for cases where goods are returned after sale because they are inadequate, damaged or over-supplied.

**Purchases returns and allowances journal** for returns to suppliers.

These special journals do not cover every transaction, so a **general journal** is kept as a grab-all for any other transactions, such as credit purchase of a fixed asset.

3   **Ledgers.** In the general ledger there is an account for every asset, liability, owners' equity item, revenue item and expense of the business. When information is posted (transferred) from journals to ledgers it is converted into debits and credits, which is the accounting way of dealing with the double entry. We shall look at this process in a little more detail soon.

As well as a general ledger, firms need special ledgers. Your general ledger account for debtors will tell you that they owe you $2 million, but you need more information than this, don't you? You need to know who they are so that you can send bills out to them. Therefore you'll have a debtors' ledger with an account for each individual debtor. The total of all these accounts in the debtors' ledger should equal the balance shown in the debtors account in the general ledger. A similar system will be used for creditors with a creditors ledger.

4   **Trial balance.** Periodically (daily, weekly, monthly, depending upon the business) the ledger accounts are balanced and the balance figures are listed to see that the system still balances. This listing is called a trial balance. Reconciliations are then carried out to correct errors. It is from this trial balance that the final reports are produced.

5   **Final reports.** The final reports are the end product of the accounting system, the reason for doing all of this processing of information. The major reports are:

- the balance sheet, which we've already looked at briefly;
- the profit and loss statement, to show revenue and expenses and the profit or loss made when they are matched together;
- the funds statement, which shows where funds have come from and how they have been used.

## How Transactions Are Processed through the System

Information is transferred into the ledger as debits and credits. To understand the full implications of this, you must understand a little about funds. Consider the simple balance sheet in Figure 2.2.

**Figure 2.2**
**FRANKIES STORES**
Balance Sheet as at 30 June 19--

| ASSETS | $ | EQUITIES | $ |
|---|---|---|---|
| Cash | 8 000 | Creditors | 4 000 |
| Debtors | 2 000 | Owners' equity | |
| Stock | 7 000 | Capital | 21 000 |
| Equipment | 8 000 | | |
| TOTAL ASSETS | $25 000 | TOTAL EQUITIES | $25 000 |

The person running Frankies Stores could make all sorts of decisions about what to do with the assets. There could be a decision to use some of the cash to buy more equipment; to sell some of the equipment and get more cash; or to use cash to buy more stock. These are decisions that re-arrange the resources in some way.

The $25,000 worth of value shown by total assets represents a body of value which can be shuffled about in a variety of ways. This amount of value at the disposal of the owner or owners is called 'funds'. The amount of funds available is limited by the equities. If the owner bought $2,000 more stock on credit the stock would increase by $2,000, creditors would increase to $6,000 and the balance sheet would now add up to $27 000. Funds available will have been increased by $2,000.

As we have already discussed, the structure of the accounting equation means that every time a transaction occurs there are two effects on the balance sheet (the double entry). One effect provides funds, the other uses funds.

You don't have to know anything about accounting to work out the following examples. Let's consider some transactions and look at the two effects on balance sheet items and movements of funds.

**Transaction 1** - Bought stock for $500 cash.

(a) The cash goes down by $500. The store of cash is the source from which funds come.

(b) The stock goes up by $500. The funds are used in increasing the stock level. The total resources (or funds) available does not change. What changes is the form in which the value is held. We had $500 worth of cash; now we have $500 worth of stock.

**Transaction 2** - Received $1000 from debtors.

(a) The debtors figure goes down by $1,000. The reduction in the asset provides some funds to be used somewhere.

(b) The cash goes up by $1,000. The funds received from reducing debtors are used to increase the holdings of cash.

**Transaction 3** - More equipment is bought for $2,000 cash.

(a) The cash goes down by $2,000. This is the source of the funds which are to be used in some other way.

(b) The equipment asset goes up by $2,000. The funds are used up by increasing this asset.

**Transaction 4** - Stock is bought on credit for $1,500.

(a) The creditors figure increases by $1,500. This is the source of the funds. Funds are increased by increasing the debts owed.

(b) The stock increases by $1,500. The extra funds are used in increasing the stock.

**Transaction 5** - Stock costing $1,000 is sold for $1,800 cash.

(a) The cash goes up by $1,800. The funds raised are used to increase the cash balance.

(b) The stock goes down by $1,000. So $1,000 of the funds comes from a decrease in the stock. And in this case there is more.

(c) There is an $800 profit which is added to owners' equity.

The profit is the source of this $800 in funds.

## The Rules of Debit and Credit

You can see that every time a transaction takes place, there is a source of funds and a use of the funds. The golden rules are that in any transaction, the part where the funds are used is called the debit (abbreviation DR), and the part of the transaction which provides the funds is called a credit (abbreviation CR). These rules are summarised in diagram form in Figure 2.3.

**Figure 2.3**

|               | INCREASE | DECREASE |
| ------------- | -------- | -------- |
| Asset         | Debit    | Credit   |
| Liability     | Credit   | Debit    |
| Owners' equity | Credit   | Debit    |

If an asset is increased by the transaction, that asset receives a debit for the amount. If the transaction increases a liability, that liability will receive a credit, and so on. Most accountants just learn this set of rules off by heart and don't worry about why it is a debit or a credit.

Much of the confusion over debit and credit experienced by the non-accountant arises out of equating ledger accounts with bank statements, where credits are desirable. They are not the same thing. A bank statement is prepared from the point of view of the bank. If you have money in the bank, the bank owes that amount to you. From their point of view, your account is a liability. Therefore, you have a **credit** balance. The use of debit and credit here must not be confused with bank usage.

As we said earlier, each of those items in the balance sheet has a ledger account. Ledger accounts are always structured so that they allow for putting debits and credits in different parts of the account. A ledger account is usually structured like the one shown in Figure 2.4.

**Figure 2.4**

| (i) | (ii) | (iii) | (iv) | (v) |
|---|---|---|---|---|
| DATE | DETAILS | DEBIT | CREDIT | BALANCE |
|  |  |  |  |  |

The name of the other account affected will go in column (ii). Debit entries go in column (iii), credit entries go in column (iv). The balance column (v) shows the net value of the entries made in the account. Returning to the transactions we looked at earlier, the debits and credits would be as follows:

**Transaction 1**

(a) Cash, credit $500

(b) Stock, debit $500

**Transaction 2**

(a) Debtors, credit $1000

(b) Cash, debit $1000

**Transaction 3**

(a) Cash credit $2000

(b) Equipment, debit $2000

**Transaction 4**

(a) Creditors, credit $1500

(b) Stock, debit $1500

**Transaction 5**

(a) Cash, debit $1800

(b) Stock, credit $1000

(c) Owners' equity, credit $800

As you can see, in every case the debit entries equal the credit entries. You can also see that after every transaction the accounting equation will balance because there are equal effects on the assets side and equities side.

Just to prove that this is true, we'll put the five transactions into the ledger accounts (Figure 2.5).

**Figure 2.5**
**Cash Account**

|  |  | DR ($) | CR ($) | BAL. ($) |
|---|---|---|---|---|
|  | Opening balance |  |  | 8 000 DR |
| 1(a) | Stock |  | 500 | 7 500 DR |
| 2(b) | Debtors | 1 000 |  | 8 500 DR |
| 3(a) | Equipment |  | 2 000 | 6 500 DR |
| 5(a) | Stock and owner's equity | 1 800 |  | 8 300 DR |

**Debtors Account**

|  |  | DR ($) | CR ($) | BAL. ($) |
|---|---|---|---|---|
|  | Opening balance |  |  | 2 000 DR |
| 2(a) | Cash |  | 1 000 | 1 000 DR |

**Stock Account**

|  |  | DR ($) | CR ($) | BAL. ($) |
|---|---|---|---|---|
|  | Opening balance |  |  | 7 000 DR |
| 1(b) | Cash | 500 |  | 7 500 DR |
| 4(b) | Creditors | 1 500 |  | 9 000 DR |
| 5(b) | Cash |  | 1 000 | 8 000 DR |

**Equipment Account**

|  |  | DR ($) | CR ($) | BAL. ($) |
|---|---|---|---|---|
|  | Opening balance |  |  | 8 000 DR |
| 3(b) | Cash | 2 000 |  | 10 000 DR |

**Creditors Account**

|  |  | DR ($) | CR ($) | BAL. ($) |
|---|---|---|---|---|
|  | Opening balance |  |  | 4000 CR |
| 4(a) | Stock |  | 1500 | 5500 CR |

**Capital Account**

|  |  | DR ($) | CR ($) | BAL. ($) |
|---|---|---|---|---|
|  | Opening balance |  |  | 21 000 CR |
| 5(c) | Cash |  | 800 | 21 800 CR |

The opening balance figure in each ledger account is the balance shown in the balance sheet. That's why it's called a balance sheet - it is a sheet showing the balances. From the ledger accounts we can construct a trial balance (Figure 2.6).

**Figure 2.6**
**Trial Balance**

|  | DR ($) | CR ($) |
|---|---|---|
| Cash | 8 300 |  |
| Debtors | 1 000 |  |
| Stock | 8 000 |  |
| Equipment | 10 000 |  |
| Creditors |  | 5 500 |
| Capital |  | 21 800 |
|  | $27 300 | $27 300 |

Since the trial balance balances, we would then make out the new balance sheet which would have the same structure as before with these new figures.

That really is all there is to the bookkeeping part of accounting.

This entering of transactions, and completing the accounting cycle, used to represent a large proportion of the accountant's work. These days, this work is done by bookkeepers, largely by computer. Accountants are involved mainly in analysis and problem solving.

You will realise that if a transaction was left out of the processing completely, the accounts would still balance. If an entry was made to the debit or credit side as required, but was put in the wrong account, it would still balance. Such an error may go unrecognised for years.

At this stage it would be a good idea to look at your own company's balance sheet to see if you can recognise each of the items mentioned. Most large companies make copies of their annual reports available to the employees. If you have your own business, your accountant should be regularly supplying you with reports. In the next chapter our magical mystery tour of the jargon of accounting continues as we drift into the morass of profit calculation. However, your confidence in the figures you see in accounting reports as a basis for making decisions should already be a little dented.

# 3

# More Basic Jargon: The Profit and Loss Statement

There's one in every bunch.

'Gee, you accountants must be thick. You can't have both a profit and loss statement. Don't you mean a profit or loss statement? Ha, ha, ha.'

Of course he is right, and every time it happens I go away determined to use my influence to get it changed. You can see how much influence I've got. Everybody still calls it a profit and loss statement. What the statement does is show the profit or loss made in a particular period, usually a financial year, and how much of the profit has been distributed to the shareholders as dividends.

## The Profit and Loss Statement

**Turnover or sales** is the first item shown in the profit and loss statement. If you are a marketer you know what that means. After all, you are one of the front-line troops in the war to generate this figure.

As you can see from Figure 3.1, usually the statement shows no details of the expenses that are deducted to reach the next figure - the operating profit before income tax, except for details of some specific minor expenses in a supplementary note. When the income tax expense is deducted, we have the operating profit after tax but before extraordinary items.

**Extraordinary items** are those which are totally outside the usual scope of the company's business. Before the requirement was introduced to show extraordinary items separately, many investors were relieved of their money by unscrupulous people hiding behind a lack of disclosure of important information. It was possible, for instance, for a company to sell off most of its plant or factories, include the capital profits made as part of the usual profits, and show a large profit figure, not disclosing that it no longer had the capacity to make profits in the next year. Now extraordinary items like that must be shown as a separate figure. Once this adjustment is made we have the operating profit.

The retained earnings of previous years are added to this figure to give the amount available for appropriation. In theory this is the total amount that the company could hand out to its shareholders as dividends. When the dividends paid are deducted, there is a retained earnings figure carried forward. This will be shown as a reserve in the balance sheet. It is the only item that appears in both the balance sheet and profit and loss statement.

At this stage we should consider an actual set of figures. These are the profit and loss statement and balance sheet of Templestowe Trading Ltd for the year ended 30 June 1989 (Figure 3.1). As you can see, there is a distinct lack of detail shown in the profit and loss statement, and although supplementary notes must show details of certain expenses, there will usually be no details of the major expenses like wages, salaries and raw material costs. It is not surprising that a clever person once said that a profit and loss statement is like a bikini swimsuit: what it reveals is interesting, but what it conceals is vital.

**Figure 3.1**
**TEMPLESTOWE TRADING LTD**
Profit and Loss Statement for the year ended 30 June 1989

|  | 1988 | 1989 |
|---|---|---|
|  | $'000 | $'000 |
| SALES | 3 240 | 2 900 |
| Operating profit before tax | 940 | 820 |
| Less: Income tax expense | 460 | 400 |
| Operating profit before extraordinary item | 480 | 420 |
| Less: Extraordinary item | 32 | — |
| OPERATING PROFIT | 448 | 420 |
| Retained earnings brought forward | 640 | 988 |
| Available for appropriation | 1 088 | 1 408 |
| Less: Dividends paid (10 cents) | 100 | 100 |
| Retained earnings carried forward | 988 | 1 308 |

## The Balance Sheet

The balance sheet is no better because as we have already seen there is not much detail and the figures are usually totally unrelated to market value for fixed assets. Figure 3.2 is a very simple example but it will give us some idea of the way these reports may be used by investors, employees and managers, despite the shortcomings we have already noted.

**Figure 3.2**
**TEMPLESTOWE TRADING LTD**
**Balance Sheet as at 30 June 1989**

|  | 1988 |  | 1989 |  |
|---|---|---|---|---|
|  | $'000 | $'000 | $'000 | $'000 |
| *Current assets* |  |  |  |  |
| Cash at bank | 28 |  | 100 |  |
| Accounts receivable | 860 |  | 1 131 |  |
| Inventory | 1 064 | 1 952 | 1 215 | 2 446 |
| *Fixed assets* |  |  |  |  |
| Plant and equipment | 960 |  | 960 |  |
| Less: Accumulated depreciation | 420 | 540 | 560 | 400 |
| TOTAL ASSETS |  | 2 492 |  | 2 846 |
| *Current liabilities* |  |  |  |  |
| Accounts payable | 360 |  | 404 |  |
| Wages owing | 34 | 394 | 22 | 426 |
| *Long-term liabilities* |  |  |  |  |
| Provisions for long service leave |  | 110 |  | 112 |
| *Share capital and reserves* |  |  |  |  |
| Authorised capital |  |  |  |  |
| (2 million $1 ordinary shares) | 2 000 | — | 2 000 | — |
| Issued and paid-up capital |  |  |  |  |
| (1 million $1 ordinary shares) |  | 1 000 |  | 1 000 |
| Retained earnings |  | 988 |  | 1 308 |
| TOTAL EQUITIES |  | 2 492 |  | 2 846 |

Despite their brevity, we can discover some important facts from these statements. From the profit and loss statement we can see that:

1 This year's sales are substantially lower than last year's sales. Investors, lenders of money to the company, employees and management should regard this as a danger signal that all is not well.

2 This year's profit is also substantially lower than the previous year's, which is not surprising with lower sales.

3 Despite the lower profit the company has still expanded because only a small dividend has been paid to the

shareholders. Their 10 cents per share represents $100,000 out of $448,000 in profits in 1988, and $100,000 out of $420,000 in profits in 1989. Provided the shareholders are willing to accept this low level of distribution of profits, the company can continue to expand with even lower profits. The effect of paying out only $100,000 in dividends out of $420,000 profits is to expand company assets by $320,000 without further financing cost. It would be wrong, however, to say that there is no cost in using these undistributed profits to finance expansion. There is always the opportunity cost, that is, the benefit that could have been gained by using the money in some other way.

From the balance sheet we can see that:

1 Despite the lower sales, accounts receivable are much greater. Unless this is the result of a conscious policy to grant longer credit terms, this should not happen. Accounts receivable earn nothing as an investment; they come into existence as a result of credit sales. Selling on credit is a marketing tool. You only do it because if you did not the customers would buy from somebody else. The funds tied up in these extra accounts receivable could be used for something more productive.

2 Despite the lower sales, inventory has become larger. This would also seem to indicate poor management. Inventory is another non-productive asset and should be kept to an efficient minimum. There is no reason why inventory should be allowed to become greater when sales are lower.

3 Cash at bank is more than three times its level of last year. This is another non-productive asset which should be kept to a minimum required for efficient conduct of the business.

4 Despite the growth in unproductive assets, the only productive assets, plant and equipment, have not been expanded at all. They are running down as they

depreciate. All of the funds for expansion provided by the profits retained in the business are being squandered by poor management of the assets. If those funds were used to purchase more plant and equipment, more goods might be handled and more sales made.

## The Funds Statement

A lot of what we have just discovered would be more obvious if we prepared a funds statement. A funds statement analyses the movement of funds for the year. It is prepared from two successive balance sheets and shows a summary of where funds came from and what funds were used for. In the case of Templestowe Trading Ltd, the funds statement would appear as in Figure 3.3.

**Figure 3.3**
**TEMPLESTOWE TRADING LTD**
**Funds Statement for the year ended 30 June 1989 ($'000)**

Funds were provided from the following sources:
1 Funds from trading:
| | | |
|---|---|---|
| Revenue received | $2 900 | |
| Less: expenses requiring funds | 2 440 | 460 |

2 Increases in liabilities:
| | | |
|---|---|---|
| Accounts payable | 44 | |
| Provision for long service leave | 2 | 46 |

TOTAL FUNDS DERIVED — $506

These funds were applied as follows:
1 Increases in assets:
| | | |
|---|---|---|
| Cash at bank | 72 | |
| Accounts receivable | 271 | |
| Inventory | 151 | 494 |

2 Decrease in liability:
| | | |
|---|---|---|
| Wages owing | | 12 |

TOTAL FUNDS APPLIED — $506

This funds statement was prepared from the two balance sheets of Templestowe Trading Ltd for 1988 and 1989. The figures are derived from the differences in the balance for each item from year to year. A few figures require some comment:

1. Funds from trading represents the amount of funds generated out of profits. The revenue figure comes from the profit and loss statement. Expenses requiring funds are all of those where an actual payment is made. The big exception is depreciation. Remember that depreciation is only a convenient way of spreading cost in calculating profit. No money is actually paid out for it, so no funds move out of the business. Therefore it is not counted.

2. Most of the funds were provided out of profit, which is a very healthy situation. We would not like to see most of the funds being provided by selling off assets or increasing liabilities.

3. Most of the funds provided, an amount greater than the funds from trading, have been used to increase the current assets.

    This is not a healthy sign as they are unproductive. We would be happier to see the funds being put into productive assets like plant and equipment.

As you can see, we can learn a lot from the funds statement as it tells us in a nutshell how successful trading operations have been and what the company has done with the profits. In one analysis course that I prepared for union shop stewards, I stressed that where funds were coming from and what was being done with them was the best indication of whether a company could afford to improve working conditions and pay higher wages. Yes, I know I'm a mercenary traitor to the cause.

See how much we could discover about the company though we have only the barest of details. Just one point before we finish with Templestowe Trading Ltd. Whose fault is the downturn in sales? Is it a marketing problem, a general management problem or perhaps a finance problem? We would need more information than we have here to find the answer, but maybe the sales manager is not as effective as he might be. Which gives me an excuse for the following story.

A keen hunter rented a dog to help him and had a wonderful day's hunting. So the next time he went hunting he asked to rent the same dog again. He had to describe the dog because he had forgotten to ask its name.

'Oh, you want Salesman,' said the owner. 'He's so good that we've raised his rate from $20 to $30.'

'The hunter paid the fee anyway and had another great day. When he went hunting again he asked for Salesman.

'Oh, we now call him "Super Salesman" and he costs $50 a day,' said the owner. The hunter paid the fee and still found the payment worthwhile.

The next time the hunter arrived to pick up the dog the owner greeted him sadly.

'Sorry I'm afraid you can't have your favourite dog this time.'

'Why not?' asked the hunter.

'Well' said the owner, 'we were so pleased with him that the other day we made the mistake of naming him "Sales Manager". Now all he will do is sit on his tail and bark.'

# 4

# Financing the Business

Do you want to know how to start a business without any capital? You find a shop which has been empty for some time and agree to pay the rent after you become established. You find some desperate wholesalers who will give you thirty days credit. You fill the shop with their merchandise and sell it all at a handsome profit before you have to pay for it. Once you pay for it you get more stock the same way. Brilliant, eh! There's only one problem. It won't work.

Every year more than half the new businesses set up will fail. Why? In most cases, because they are under-capitalised. There is not enough money in the bag to keep things going while the business becomes properly established. Having sufficient finance is absolutely critical.

## Equity Finance and Debt Finance

Broadly speaking, there are only two possible sources of finance. Either the owners of the business provide the money themselves, or they borrow the money from somebody else. Money provided by the owners is called equity finance. In a sole proprietorship or a partnership, this takes the form of money or other assets being given to the business by the owner or partner. In a company, equity financing consists of issuing shares. The total of equity finance is the shareholders' funds figure.

Borrowed money is called debt finance. It may consist of loans from banks or other financial institutions or loans from the general public. Before we look at the details of the various kinds of loans, it is necessary to consider the basic principles of finance. No, it's not true that the only principle is to rip off what you can, where you can.

## The Risk-Free Rate

The rate which underpins all interest rates is referred to as the risk-free rate. There are investments that are entirely risk-free. That is, there is no possibility of losing the amount invested. A good example is Treasury Bonds. These are issued by the federal government with a guarantee of interest and repayment on specified dates. A change of the party in power, difficult economic conditions and fluctuating interest rates make no difference. You know what you will get and when you will get it. If the government is issuing Treasury Notes with a 10 per cent rate of interest, you can invest in them and get 10 per cent per annum without taking any risks at all.

Since investment in any business has certain risks, all investors in the business will require that risk-free rate plus some extra reward for taking risks. Back in the 1960s the risk-free rate was only about 4 per cent per annum. The major reason for the increase is the effect of inflation. If the inflation rate is about 6 per cent per annum, this has to be built into the rates offered so that the investors make real gains.

## The Premium for Risk

The amount above the risk-free rate which an investor receives for taking risk is called the premium for risk. The premium for risk varies according to the perceived degree of risk in the investment. There are two major kinds of risk;

- Income risk. This is the risk that the returns from the investment will not be as god as expected; and
- Capital risk. This is the risk that you will lose the capital that you have invested.

Clearly capital risk is more serious than income risk. The risk-free rate rewards investors for the time that they defer personal use of their money by letting others use it. The premium for risk rewards the investor for taking the risks. The greater the degree of risk, the greater must be the possible rewards for taking that risk.

From this we can draw some general rules.

- The greater the risk, the greater the potential return must be to compensate for that risk.
- The lower the risk, the lower the return.
- No business investment is worthwhile unless it returns greater than the risk-free rate.

Therefore, businesses involved in high-risk activities such as minerals exploration, oil drilling and land development will probably be required to offer higher returns than those in safer activities like food retailing, banking and oil refining.

## The Opportunity Rate

An investor will check a potential investment against other investments with a similar level of risk. The best return offered for that degree of risk is referred to as the opportunity rate. It is the yardstick against which an investment will be measured. If the investment offered does not match that potential return for the level of risk, it will not attract investors. So in trying to raise finance, a business must at least match the investors' opportunity rate.

## Aversion to Risk

Surveys of investor behavior indicate that investors are risk averse. That is, they do not like to take risks. This should not be particularly surprising to you. It's one thing to have a bit of a dabble on the horses occasionally, but it's something else again to blow $50,000 in somebody else's business failure. You don't even get to watch them run. So investors will rarely take chances for the thrill of it all.

## The Golden Rule of Finance

One of the golden rules of finance is to finance short-term needs by short-term methods and long-term needs by long-term methods. So, if you need temporary funds to boost stock levels for Christmas or to pay Christmas bonuses or to purchase raw materials at discount prices, you should use a short-term borrowing method such as bank overdraft. There is little point in paying interest on the money for long periods when you don't really need it. Added to this, long-term interest rates tend to be higher than short-term rates. Bank overdraft is generally available only on a short-term basis and it is usually the cheapest money available to you.

On the other hand, if you want to purchase more plant which will increase production and profits over the next ten years, then it would make sense to finance the plant over ten years. To finance this long-term asset on a series of renewed short-term loans would be more expensive because of the charges made to establish each loan. There is also a possibility of great fluctuations in the short-term interest rate. With a long-term loan you could more effectively budget for your commitments.

## Effects of Tax Deductibility of Interest Payments

All of the legitimate expenses of earning taxable income are tax-deductible. Therefore, the net cost of those expenses to the business is reduced by the amount of tax saving. **Interest on borrowed money is a tax-deductible expense** so the net cost of borrowing money is much lower than the rate of interest nominated.

Assume that Alpha Ltd has taken out a loan of $300,000 to buy equipment. The loan has been made from a trading bank at 18 per cent per annum. So the annual interest payable is 18 per cent of $300,000 which equals $54,000.

However, let us assume that the taxation rate paid on profits made is 39 cents in the dollar, as it currently is for companies. The company would use the $54,000 interest paid as a tax deduction, and would save $54,000 multiplied by 39 cents in tax payable, that is $21,060. So the net cost of borrowing the money is $54,000 less $21,060, which equals $32,940. This represents an interest rate after tax of only 10.98 per cent.

If, on the other hand, a company used a share issue to raise the finance required, the dividends paid to shareholders are not tax-deductible because they are a distribution of profits to the owners (the shareholders) and not a business expense. Neither are distributions of profit to partners or owners.

## Gearing of Company Finance

Businesses that rely heavily on borrowed money are said to be highly geared. Because of the comparatively low after tax cost of borrowing, there is a good argument for relying mainly on borrowed money. However, there are dangers.

Lenders to a business will normally have their loans secured over some assets of the business. If their interest is not paid on the due dates, or the loan is not repaid when due, the lenders can seize those assets and sell them to get their money back. This will probably destroy the business. In times of economic boom, the earnings of a highly-geared business can make the owners very wealthy, but when economic conditions are difficult many highly-geared businesses fail because the commitment to pay interest continues even if the business makes no sales at all.

Experts (that is us, the accountants) differ on what constitutes a highly-geared company. However, few accountants would disagree that a company which uses more than 60 per cent borrowed money is highly geared. In chapter 3, Templestowe Trading Ltd at 30 June 1989 had a balance sheet which showed borrowed money (liabilities) of $538,000 and owners' equity (share capital and reserves) of $2,308,000. So out of total funds used of $2,846,000 only $538,000 or about 19 per cent was borrowed money. This makes it a low-geared business and therefore it should be secure in the long run.

## Security of Lenders and Shareholders

Another point that should be made is that if the business fails and its assets are liquidated, lenders to the business will be repaid before the shareholders receive anything on their shares. Therefore lenders enjoy a higher degree of security than owners or shareholders.

This means that following our earlier rules, the shareholders should be able to look forward to higher returns than the lenders because of their higher level of risk. From the point of view of the business, this means that equity finance is more expensive than debt finance even without the tax saving on the interest. When the tax savings are considered, generally speaking debt finance costs less than half the cost of equity finance.

## Sources of Short-Term Finance

There are various sources of short-term finance.

**Bank Overdraft** is available unsecured to well-established businesses, but most of the time good security such as a mortgage over property or a personal guarantee will be required. It has comparatively cheap interest rates and no establishment fees but bank overdraft is payable on demand from the bank, so it is not suitable for long-term purposes.

**Commercial bills** are generally available only to companies with a good credit rating. The company issues a commercial bill promising to repay the money borrowed, with interest, at a set date in the future. This is not unlike an IOU.

**Factoring** Another option is to sell the accounts receivable (or debtors) to a finance company at a discount. The business receives immediate payment for less than the book value of the debtors. This is called factoring. Finance companies are generally interested only where the business makes credit sales of at least $200,000 per annum and agrees to an ongoing arrangement. Any debts not collected must usually be refunded by the business to the finance company.

**Import and export finance** is another form of short-term finance. Financial institutions called confirming houses arrange funds so that importers do not have to pay for imported goods until about a month or so after the goods arrive in Australia. They make similar arrangements so that exporters receive payment for exports as soon as they are shipped. The actual suppliers of the funds are usually the trading banks.

**Inventory financing** or **floor plan financing** in Australia is generally available only to large businesses that act as agents of finance companies when selling their inventory. A common example is the motor car trader. Provided the trader uses the finance company concerned for its customers to finance their purchases, the finance company will finance the trader's inventory at special rates of interest. Although it tends to restrict the trader's flexibility in obtaining funds from elsewhere, it provides guaranteed finance for a major item.

**Creditors or accounts payable** is the only source of finance without an interest charge. However, if it is abused you may lose it entirely. Although accounts should be paid promptly and within the agreed terms, there is little benefit to the business in paying accounts early unless discounts are offered as an incentive.

As we have already seen, accounts receivable represent an amount of free finance that we are providing to others so it is pleasant if we can achieve a positive net credit position, that is, we have more creditors than debtors.

Suppose we have daily credit sales of $5000 and collect, on average, in thirty days. Our accounts receivable balance will average $150,000. If, on the other hand, our average daily credit purchases are $4,000 with an average payment period of twenty-five days, our average accounts payable will be only $100,000. This means that we are providing $50,000 more free credit than we receive. Changing the situation so that our average payment period is forty days will give us average accounts payable of $160,000 and a net credit position of $10,000 positive, which is a much better financial position.

The change releases $60,000 in funds for some productive purpose. Large businesses tend to be net providers of trade credit and smaller businesses net users.

## Discounts for Prompt Payment

Sometimes special discounts are given for quick payment. Usually, these should be accepted. Suppose, for instance, that the terms of payment offered are '2/10, net 30 days'. This means that a discount of 2 per cent is available if we pay within ten days. Otherwise the whole amount must be paid within thirty days. If the amount owing is $100, we can pay $98 up to the tenth day, or the full $100 on the thirtieth day. If we do not take up the discount we are paying $2 for the use of $98 for twenty more days. That may not sound like much, but converted to an annual basis it is a monstrous 36.5 per cent:

$$\frac{\$2}{98} = 2\% \text{ for 20 days}$$

Converted to an annual basis:

$$2\% \times \frac{365}{20} = 36.5\%$$

Most financing methods would provide finance at a lower rate of interest than 36.5 per cent per annum. For instance, to borrow $98 for twenty days as bank overdraft at 15 per cent per annum would cost about 80 cents, not $2. Although this does not seem like a large difference, if the debt were $100,000, the difference would be $800.

## Sources of Long-Term Finance

So far, we have considered only short-term finance. The sources of long-term finance are either equity finance or debt finance.

**Equity Finance** For the reasons already outlined, equity finance or the issue of shares should usually be a last resort. However, if the company's shares are selling at substantially more than their face value, the company may consider it worthwhile to make a share issue at a premium. It must guard against the possibility of outsiders using these shares to mount a takeover.

In practice, companies rarely use share issues solely as a means of obtaining finance. In the sole proprietorship and partnership, the equivalent of share issues is the additional contribution of capital. The owner or partner gives additional assets to the business.

**Trading bank term loans** can be provided for fixed periods of three to ten years for such things as land, buildings, plant and equipment. Banks will usually require security of some kind which is frequently a mortgage over land or other assets of the business.

**Leasing finance** is available from trading banks and finance companies for the lease of plant and equipment. The lease is usually for the 'economic' life of the goods leased. Leasing enables the lessee to use productive equipment without any outlay of capital. Interest rates tend to be a little higher than those on loans, but no deposit or contribution towards the cost is required of the lessee, other than payment of the first month's lease premium.

Changes in accounting practice, in theory at least, have ended the practice of leaving leased assets off balance sheets, but the other benefits make leasing an attractive alternative. All lease payments for business assets used in producing taxable income are tax-deductible expenses. Many companies find it profitable to sell their premises and then lease them back from the purchaser, as generally speaking depreciation on buildings is not allowable as a tax-deductible expense, but lease payments are.

**Hire-purchase** Due to restrictions by state governments hire purchase is a much less common form of finance than it used to be. Finance companies retain ownership of the asset concerned until the final payment is made. At that time ownership transfers to the hirer. Interest tends to be fairly high, as a flat rate is charged for the whole life of the contract. Usually a substantial deposit is required from the purchaser.

**Government sources of finance** Various government bodies provide finance for a number of purposes. These include Export Market Development Grants, Export Expansion Grants, State Government Decentralisation Subsidies, Commonwealth Development Bank loans and Australian Industrial Research and Development Incentives. Full lists of government sources are available from the Australian Government Publishing Service.

**Debentures** are certificates issued by companies to people who lend them money. The debenture carries a fixed rate of interest, usually paid quarterly or half-yearly, and it is repayable at a fixed date in the future. The debenture is secured over assets of the company, and a trustee is appointed to supervise the interests of the debenture holders. If the debenture is described as a 'mortgage debenture' it must be secured by a first mortgage over real estate.

**Unsecured notes** are similar to debentures except there is no security over assets of the company. This makes the risk to the investor higher so the rate of interest offered will usually be a little higher than that on the same company's debentures. Finance companies commonly use unsecured notes to obtain funds to lend to clients.

**Convertible notes** are a more recent development. They are similar to unsecured notes, except that, instead of providing for the return of the money to the lender at the date of maturity, they are convertible into an agreed number of the company's shares. There are complex taxation reasons why convertible notes may be attractive to investors.

## Calculating the Company's Cost of Capital

Having reviewed the potential sources of finance, we can now consider how a business may calculate its cost of capital. Remember we agreed earlier that all assets must be financed.

### The Cost of Debt Capital

The cost of the capital used by the company is dependent upon the rate that must be paid to lenders for debt capital and the rate which must be paid to shareholders to satisfy them and keep up the share value. However, remember also that the real cost of debt capital is the cost after a tax deduction has been claimed.

The cost of debt capital is easily measured as the rate of interest which is paid to the lender less the tax savings.

$$\text{Net cost of debt capital} = (\text{Interest rate paid}) \times (1 - \text{tax rate})$$

So, if the debt capital used is debentures with a 16 per cent rate of interest, and the taxation rate is 39 cents in the dollar, the after-tax rate of interest paid is:

$$16\% \times (1 - 0.39) = 16\% \times 0.61$$
$$= 9.76\%$$

### The Cost of Equity Capital

The cost of equity capital is more difficult to work out. What we are trying to do is to find the rate of return that will currently satisfy the shareholders, given the degree of risk that they are taking. In doing this we assume that the current yield, that is the percentage return on the shares at their market price, is acceptable to the shareholders. We presume that if it was not acceptable, the market price of the shares would have fallen. We must also include in the returns of shareholders the potential growth in future earnings.

It is essential to realise that the cost of equity capital is simply the returns to shareholders, looked at from the point of view of the company. So a simple formula for funding the cost of equity capital is.

$$Ke = \frac{D}{MP}\% + G\%$$

where Ke = cost of equity capital
D = the latest cash dividend for the year
MP = current market price per share
G = expected annual growth rate in company earnings

Therefore if a company has paid dividends of $1.20 in the past year, the current market price of its share is $10 and earnings are expected to grow at a rate of 5 per cent per annum, the cost of equity capital is:

$$Ke = \frac{\$1.20}{\$10.00}\% + 5\%$$
$$= 12\% + 5\%$$
$$= 17\%$$

Remember, this is also the total return to shareholders. If it is not in line with the level of risk to the shareholders' investment, there must be an adjustment. The rate of return above (17 per cent) is not particularly high. If there were a substantial degree of risk in investing in this company, the return would not be sufficient and an automatic adjustment would occur. Since the growth rate and the dividends are fixed as future and past events, the only variable that can adjust is the market price. So if the degree of risk in the company implies that the rate of return to shareholders should be 25 per cent, the share price would drop until that occurred.

In this case the share price would fall over a period of time to $6. At that price the cost of equity capital (or return to shareholders) would be:

$$Ke = \frac{\$1.20}{\$6.00}\% + 5\%$$
$$= 20\% + 5\%$$
$$= 25\%$$

So it is the level of risk in the company that determines the cost of equity capital.

We have considered the cost of capital being used by the company, looking at both the debt capital and the equity capital. To get the overall average cost of capital used we must calculate those rates, but they must be weighted so that we take into consideration the quantity of each type of capital used. In other words, we need the weighted average cost of capital.

For example, Wallaby Trading Ltd has been financed by the issue of 12 per cent debentures and ordinary shares. There are $300,000 worth of debentures and 700,000 $1 ordinary shares. Currently these shares are selling at $2.50 each; the last year's dividends are 40 cents in total per share; the growth rate is 6 per cent. The tax rate is 39 cents per dollar.

$$\text{Cost of debt capital} = 12\% \times (1 - 0.39)$$
$$= 12\% \times 0.61$$
$$= 7.3\%$$

$$\text{Cost of equity capital} = \frac{0.40}{2.50}\% + 6\%$$
$$= 16\% + 6\%$$
$$= 22\%$$

Total capital used at present is:

$$\text{Debt capital} = \$300\,000$$

$$\text{Equity capital} = \$700\,000 \times \$2.50 = \$1\,750\,000$$

$$\text{Total capital used} = \$300\,000 + 1\,750\,000 = \$2\,050\,000$$

Proportion of debt and equity capital used is:

$$\text{Debt capital} = \frac{300\,000}{2\,050\,000} = 14.6\% \text{ or } 0.146$$

$$\text{Equity capital} = \frac{1\,750\,000}{2\,050\,000} = 85.4\% \text{ or } 0.854$$

To find the weighted average cost of capital all we need to do is apply the proportionate weights to the rates we calculated earlier:

| (a) Type of Capital | (b) Value of Capital | (c) After Tax Rate % | (d) Weight | (e) Cost of Capital % |
|---|---|---|---|---|
| Debt | $300,000 | 7.3% | 0.146 | 1.0658 |
| Equity | $1,750,000 | 22.0% | 0.854 | 18.7880 |
| | | Weighted average cost of capital | | 19.8538% |

Column (c) is the after-tax cost of each kind of capital; (d) is the proportionate weight of each; (e) is the result of (c) x (d).

The weighted average cost of capital is just under 20 per cent. So any existing asset must produce a rate of return of at least 20 per cent. If it does not, the cost of the capital used is greater than the returns produced and the asset should be disposed of if it is not possible to improve the situation.

Heavy stuff, isn't it? You can see why accountants get so excited about the rate of return expected of a new line or a new plant. You can also see why they're so fussy about predictions for sales. Those sales predictions are the basis on which future cash flows are estimated as a basis for predicting returns. If they are substantially wrong, then the wrong decision may be made. Although it is not wise to be too optimistic, neither should you be too restricted in your ambition.

You may have heard about the sales manager who was boasting in a speech he was giving about the efficiency of his sales organisation.

'We've got things really buzzing to the stage where we're making a sale every three minutes of every day', he said proudly.

'Not enough', came a voice from the floor.

The sales manager ignored the interruption, and continued.

'With our new promotions and a direct mail campaign we expect to rapidly reach the stage where we're making a sale every two minutes.'

'Still not enough', the voice repeated.

The sales manager was livid. He picked the man out and barked, 'Look, you've interrupted me twice. Now explain to me why making a sale every two minutes is still not enough.'

'Certainly', came the reply. 'There's a sucker born every minute.'

# 5

# Planning to Make Profits

There's an old saying that you may have heard: If you want to know what God thinks of money, look at the people He gives it to. That may be true but it does not alter the fact that people are in business to make profits. As we have already seen, investment in a business relies on the perception that there is a profit to be made. Anyone who has managed to make it through primary school can work out whether a profit has been made after it has all happened. The difficult part is to assess the situation in advance and plan for profits. This requires a knowledge of likely sales, cost structure and resources available.

## Sales Planning

When we talk about sales planning, we are taking things a little further than sales forecasting. A forecast is largely a statistical exercise that implies continuity of past activities. A plan implies that there will be new decisions or at least a reassessment of the existing approach. In planning to make profits we must have a full understanding of the sales forecast; the profit targets; and the cost structure of the business.

## Sales Forecasting

Broadly speaking there are two different approaches to sales forecasting: macroforecasting and microforecasting.

They may be used separately or in conjunction. As usual, the pretentious names cover up simple ideas.

**Macroforecasting** concentrates on looking at the market as a whole. A number of techniques are used, but two common ones are **demand analysis** and **market-share forecasting**. Demand analysis involves estimating a demand curve for the item concerned. This requires that the likely sales levels be determined for each selling price. Economic, psychological and competitor factors come into the analysis. The economic factors include the impact on the product of changes in customers' disposable income due to such effects as tax changes; and the cost savings which may result from using the product.

One example often quoted of this kind of economic interrelationship is the situation where potato prices rise suddenly. When this happens some potential buyers of potatoes will switch to rice or another substitute. If this continues, the increased demand for rice will start to push rice prices up also.

Psychological factors are also important. Is the product attractive in itself or attractively packaged? Does it grant some status to the purchaser? In attempts to influence these psychological factors, businesses spend millions on product design, promotions, packaging and advertising. All marketers are conscious of the importance of advertising. As a young keen accountant running around trying to slash costs, I was once told by a battle-scarred veteran of the marketing wars, 'Cutting down on advertising to save money is like stopping your watch to save time.'

Competitive factors are also important. If potential customers can buy exactly the same product at a cheaper price from your competitor, they won't recognise any obligation to keep you in business. However, it is possible to compete on grounds other than price. If price was all that mattered we would all buy weatherboard houses in small country towns, drive second-hand wrecks from the 1960s, be dressed by the St Vincent de Paul Society and live on stale bread and pet food. Other things matter such as location, status, convenience, safety and quality. It is possible to sell rather ordinary products at very high prices with the right kind of promotion.

Problems in estimating the psychological and competitive factors with any degree of accuracy make demand curve construction difficult, but where demand curves can be calculated, they can be valuable aids to profit planning and pricing.

Another macroforecasting technique is market-share analysis. This is simple:

Step 1: Assess the current size of the market and your market share.

Step 2: Estimate next year's growth of the total market.

Step 3: Assume that you will maintain the same market share.

Step 4: Apply the percentage in Step 3 to the estimate made in Step 2.

Easy, eh? Like all easy things it doesn't work particularly well. It's great if you are a major producer, there are only a few competitors and the product is well established. Otherwise it's about as scientific and precise as performing an appendectomy with a chainsaw. So if the answer is not in macroforecasting it must be in microforecasting. Or is it?

**Microforecasting** simply means finding out a lot of little bits and putting them together to get an overall figure. Often it is suggested that sales representatives could approach customers to ask what they are likely to purchase in future periods. This sounds fine in theory but in practice it is often unrealistic. Customers may not have a particularly good idea of their future intentions, or they may not want you to know about their future intentions. They may buy from several sources and you may have only a part of their business. They may also think it rather strange that you don't know what you are doing! So you may be left to rely on the estimates of sales representatives and these are notoriously unreliable.

In practice, firms often use a combination of both macro- and microforecasting. Two imperfect methods do not make a perfect one, but by using both there is a lessened chance of gross inaccuracy. It must be admitted that in many cases sales departments just take the previous year's figures and add on a percentage based on an educated guess. This 'by guess and by God' method has little to recommend it - other than simplicity.

## Calculating a Target Profit

In chapter 4 we saw that it was possible to find the cost of equity capital - the percentage return expected by shareholders, or the rate of return that a company must pay to maintain its share prices. We can use this cost of equity capital to find the after-tax target profit required:

After-tax target profit = Cost of equity capital x Market value of equity capital

Take, for instance, the well-known grunch manufacturer, Supergrunch Ltd. Their cost of equity capital is 20 per cent, and the capital consists of 100,000 shares with a market value of $6 each. So the after-tax target profit (ATP) required is:

ATP = 0.20 x 100 000 x $6
    = $120 000

This means that the company must make an after-tax profit of $120,000 in order to satisfy the shareholders. If it makes less than this amount in after-tax profit, the shareholders will not receive the 20 per cent rate of return commensurate with the degree of risk they are taking. As we have seen, this will probably mean that the market price of the shares will drop until a 20 per cent return is possible.

However, the after-tax profit is not our true target, as the profit made must be great enough to pay the tax and leave the desired after-tax profit for the shareholders. To convert the after-tax target profit to before-tax target profit we use the formula:

$$\text{Before-tax target profit} = \frac{\text{After-tax target profit}}{1 - \text{tax rate}}$$

In the above case, if the tax rate is 39 cents in the dollar as it is for Australian companies, the before-tax target profit must be:

$$\text{Before-tax target profit} = \frac{\$120\,000}{1 - 0.39}$$
$$= \$196\,721$$

If the company makes a before-tax target profit of $196,721, this will provide enough profit to pay the tax of $76,721 and leave $120,000 for the shareholders. So this company's target must be to make a before-tax profit of $196,721.

The other piece of information required is the cost structure for production of the product. In particular, we need to know the amount of fixed and variable costs which must be spent.

## Fixed and Variable Costs

**Fixed costs** are costs that remain constant as the volume of production changes. Whether the business produces hundreds of units, or no units at all, the amount of cost will be the same. Some good examples of fixed costs are rent of a factory, council rates and depreciation. It is obvious that at a particular level any fixed cost may have to be increased. Factory rent, for instance, will increase if production goes beyond the capacity of the existing factory so that we need another factory. In order to prevent this problem affecting the analysis, we restrict our analysis to the range of production that can be handled by existing facilities. This is called the **relevant range**.

**Variable costs** are those which increase or decrease **in direct proportion to the volume of production or sales**. The implication of 'direct proportion' is that there is a constant relationship between level of production or sales and cost. If the level of production doubles, the cost doubles. If the level of production is cut by a third, the cost will be cut by a third. The most obvious examples of variable costs are raw material costs, sales commissions and factory wages. I know that economists might like to argue about this because they will talk about economies of scale and the law of diminishing returns. However, for costs like raw materials there is a close approximation to directly proportionate cost, particularly when you consider that we are only talking about what is happening within a relevant range.

**Semi-variable** costs are those which contain an element of both fixed and variable costs. There are many costs of this type. A complex example is the cost of sales representatives' vehicles. Registration, insurance and disposal costs are fixed, but fuel, maintenance and tyres are variable. A simpler example is the rent for a shop in a shopping complex where the cost often contains a fixed weekly amount plus a small percentage of turnover. In all semi-variable costs, it is possible to use analysis techniques to isolate the fixed and variable elements in the cost. This is important because the reliability of cost analysis relies on the accurate separation into fixed and variable costs.

Let's assume that Supergrunch Ltd can do this and we have calculated that in manufacturing and selling grunches fixed costs are $50,000, and that there is a variable cost to make and sell of $2 per grunch. We are certain that we can sell the product at $6 a unit.

## The Contribution Margin

Consider the relationship of these figures. Every unit we can make and sell produces a potential profit of $4, once we have sold enough to pay the fixed costs. Until then the $4 contributes towards meeting the fixed costs. For this reason the selling price less the variable cost is called the **contribution margin**. That is:

Contribution margin (CM) = Selling price (SP) − Variable cost (VC)

In our example:

$$\begin{aligned} CM &= SP - VC \\ &= \$6 - \$2 \\ &= \$4 \text{ per unit} \end{aligned}$$

## The Break-Even Point

We will not make profits until sufficient contribution margin has been accumulated to cover the fixed costs. At that point there will be no profit and no loss on the product. This level of sales is called the **break-even point**. The break-even point in unit sales is easily obtained by dividing the fixed costs by the contribution margin per unit. So:

$$\text{Break-even point (B/E)} = \frac{\text{Fixed costs of the product (FC)}}{\text{Contribution margin per unit (CM)}}$$

In our example:

$$\begin{aligned} B/E &= \frac{FC}{CM \text{ per unit}} \\ &= \frac{\$50\,000}{\$4} \\ &= 12\,500 \text{ units} \end{aligned}$$

When 12,500 grunches are sold for $6 each, with the cost structure mentioned earlier, neither a profit nor a loss is made. Beyond that break-even point, every unit sold will contribute $4 to the profit. So production and sale of 20,500 units, for instance, would provide a profit of 20,500 less 12,500, which equals 8000 units, multiplied by $4 contribution margin, which equals $32 000.

Using the techniques that we have now mastered (well some of us have anyway), we can calculate the number of units that must be sold to provide the before-tax profit required. Earlier we said that Supergrunch Ltd needed to make a before-tax profit of $196,721. We can calculate reasonably easily how many units this requires. We have already calculated that it requires sale of 12,500 units to break even. So we need those, plus enough to give us another $196,721. Since each grunch provides $4 towards that profit, we need to make and sell:

$$\frac{\$196\,721}{\$4} = 49\,180$$

above the break-even point. That is, we must make and sell 12,500 plus 49,180, which equals 61,680 units. If we can do that we will make the before-tax target profit of $196,721, pay the tax and make the earnings required to keep up the value of the shares.

If this all seems a little simplified then your instincts are right. Nothing is ever quite that simple. However, in the next chapter we will take the break-even concept and give it a few complications so that you can appreciate the way in which the concept can be extended nearer to the more complex realities of life.

# 6

# Into the Heart of Break-Even Analysis

There is not much fun in being in business if you don't make profits. In fact, business has been defined as the art of extracting money from people without actually resorting to violence. The cost, volume and profit analysis in the previous chapter can ensure that profits are maximised by enabling managers to assess the variables affecting profit, and also examine the impact on profit of changes in these variables.

## The Contribution Margin Ratio

You will recall that the contribution margin is the selling price of the product less its variable cost. It is often helpful to consider this as a ratio, rather than as an amount of money. Not surprisingly, this is called the **contribution margin ratio**.

The contribution margin ratio is the contribution margin expressed as a percentage of sales revenue. That is:

$$\frac{\text{Contribution margin per unit (or in total)}}{\text{Selling price per unit (or total sales revenue)}}$$

expressed as a proportion.

So in the Supergrunch Ltd example, where selling price was $6 and variable cost was $2, giving a contribution margin of $4, the contribution margin ratio is:

$$\frac{4}{6} = 0.667$$

In the previous chapter we used the contribution margin to find the break-even point in units. Similarly we can use the contribution margin ratio to find the break-even point in dollar sales.

$$\text{Break-even point in \$ sales} = \frac{\text{Fixed costs of the product}}{\text{Contribution margin ratio}}$$

In our example of Supergrunch Ltd:

$$\frac{\$50\,000}{0.667} = \$75\,000$$

This makes sense because the break-even point was 12,500 units. At $6 each selling price, this is $75,000 sales.

## Break-even Analysis for Retailers

The contribution margin ratio approach to break-even point is particularly valuable for retailers. It is the nature of retail businesses to sell a range of articles, all of which would have different selling prices and variable costs per unit. Therefore, each line has its own different contribution margin. This makes it impossible to use a per unit approach to break-even analysis.

Retailers usually treat their cost of sales as the variable cost in the calculation, deducting it from sales revenue to find the total contribution margin. This enables them to calculate a break-even point in $ Sales.

Suppose, for example, that Dingbat Trading has found that over the past year its fixed costs have been $32,000 per month and it has made sales of $960,000 with a cost of sales of $576,000.

Total contribution margin earned is, therefore:

$960,000 - $576,000 = $384,000

The contribution margin ratio is

$$\frac{\$384,000}{\$960,000} = 0.4$$

That is, 0.4 or 40% of sales revenue is contribution margin.

If fixed costs are to remain the same next year, it must make:

$$\frac{\$32,000}{0.4} = \$80,000$$

worth of sales per month to break even.

The only problem with this retailing analysis is that it assumes the sales mix and margins will not change.

## The Margin of Safety

If the break-even point is the level of sales at which losses are no longer made, any sales currently expected beyond that level can be described as the margin of safety:

Margin of safety = Current sales level – break-even point

This may be expressed either in dollars or in units.

Since companies with high levels of fixed costs have high break-even points to meet those fixed costs, they also tend to have lower margins of safety. Consider, for instance, two companies with identical turnover and identical profit, as set out in Figure 6.1.

**Figure 6.1**

|  | Delta Company | Omega Company |
|---|---|---|
| Sales | $400 000 | 400 000 |
| Less: Variable expenses | 300 000 | 200 000 |
| Contribution margin | 100 000 | 200 000 |
| Less: Fixed expenses | 60 000 | 160 000 |
| Operating profit | $40 000 | $40 000 |

The Delta Company has a contribution margin ratio of:

$$\frac{100\,000}{400\,000} = 0.25$$

So its break-even point in sales dollars is:

$$\frac{\$60\,000}{0.25} = \$240\,000$$

Whereas the Omega Company has a contribution margin ratio of:

$$\frac{\$200\,000}{400\,000} = 0.50$$

and a break-even point in sales dollars of:

$$\frac{160\,000}{0.50} = \$320\,000$$

Clearly, because of the Omega Company's comparatively higher level of fixed expenses it has a higher break-even point and a smaller margin of safety.

|  | Delta Company | Omega Company |
|---|---|---|
| Margin of safety | $400 000 − 60 000 = $340 000 | $400 000 − 160 000 = $240 000 |

## Operating Leverage

This relationship between fixed and variable costs and sales is also known as operating leverage. Operating leverage can be measured by dividing the contribution margin by the operating profit before tax. At the $400,000 sales level:

|  | Delta Company | Omega Company |
|---|---|---|
| Degree of leverage | $\frac{100\,000}{40\,000} = 2.5$ | $\frac{200\,000}{40\,000} = 5.0$ |

This means that, at this particular sales level Delta Company increases its profit by 2.5 per cent for each 1 per cent increase in sales volume. On the other hand, because of its higher fixed costs, Omega Company has a profit change of 5 per cent for each 1 per cent change in sales. On the surface of it, Omega Company is in a more favourable situation. However, remember that there is the same multiplier in operation if the sales level falls.

To summarise, companies which are highly capitalised as a result of installation of automated assembly lines or technologically advanced equipment have higher fixed costs and higher break-even points. However, provided the fixed costs are covered, profits will expand at a tremendous rate once the break-even point is passed, because of the higher contribution margin per unit due to the reduction in variable costs.

## Using Contribution Margin as a Basis for Sales Commissions

In many firms the contribution margin is used for purposes other than break-even calculation. It can be used in the calculation of sales commissions. If sales representatives are paid commissions or bonuses on the basis of sales made, there is no consideration of the profitability of those sales. If commissions are paid on the basis of contribution margin earned for the firm, there is an incentive to concentrate sales effort on the more profitable lines. Some firms take this approach a step further by deducting the sales person's travel, entertainment and other expenses from the contribution margin before calculating commission.

## Using Contribution Margin to Optimise the Sales Mix

The contribution margin can also be used in optimising sales mix. The sales mix is the particular combination of products represented in the total sales. The highest profit comes from a sales mix containing a high proportion of high-margin items. If the sales mix changes so that there is a higher proportion of low-margin items, the profit made may fall even if the total sales increase. The aim must be to sell as many items as possible with a high contribution margin. Therefore sales people should always be made aware of which items have high and low contribution margins.

## Break-Even Analysis and Proposed New Products

If a new product is proposed, break-even analysis is very useful in determining whether it is worth pursuing. In this situation, calculations will be made using the increased fixed costs necessary to the proposal, the variable cost per unit and the estimated selling price per unit.

If, for instance, a new type of sprogget is proposed, it may be that $30,000 additional fixed costs are involved in having the new product available for sale. Variable costs for the product are estimated at $3 per unit, and the selling price is estimated at $5 per unit.

$$\text{Break-even point} = \frac{\$30\,000}{\$5 - 3}$$
$$= 15\,000 \text{ units}$$

If it was believed that the selling price of $5 is too high to allow sales of 15,000 units, demand analysis may be made to see what would happen if the selling price was increased, or decreased. If, for instance, it was found that by dropping the selling price to $4, it was possible to make sales of 50,000 units, this may make the project viable, as break-even would be $30,000 fixed costs divided by the contribution margin of $1 per unit, which is 30,000 units. Total profit would be $20,000.

On the other hand, if there was an opening for a high-quality sprogget in small quantities, say 5,000 possible sales at $23 each, the break-even point would be:

$$\frac{\$30\,000}{20} = 1500 \text{ units}$$

and total profit would be $70,000. Clearly, in this case, the small volume, high-quality product would be the best alternative.

## The Learning Curve Effect

Whenever a new manufacturing situation is introduced, the workers have to learn how to perform new tasks. With experience, workers perform these tasks more quickly and with less wastage of materials. Therefore, it is likely that subsequent units of product will be produced more cheaply than the first ones made. This is called the learning curve effect. There is nothing unusual about it. Think about the first time you did anything compared with doing it now.

Much of the research in this area has been done in the aircraft construction industry. It may be noticed, for instance, that the first aircraft of a new type took 10,000 labor hours to assemble. The second one may have taken only 7,000 hours. After two aircraft have been assembled, the average assembly time is 17,000 hours divided by 2, which equals 8,500 hours.

By doubling the production, average assembly time is only 85 per cent of the time required for the first one. If production is doubled again to four units, research shows that it is likely that average production time will now be only 85 per cent of the average for two units. This would mean an average of 7,225 hours per aircraft. The learning curve effect may continue like this until very high production levels are reached. With new products, in particular, allowance must be made for the learning curve effect. It implies higher variable costs early in production runs.

This can mean that if a firm is at the forefront of producing a new product, it can sell its early production at a high price with little competition to cover the early high cost of production. As it proceeds along the learning curve, its costs per unit will decline, enabling it to sell at a lower price than new entrants to the field. This may effectively shut out competition. When break-even analysis is done, allowance should be made for lowering of costs due to the learning curve.

In practice, a number of complications arise with the break-even approach.

1. The time period selected for the analysis may affect the result. If estimates of the first year only are used, the results may be quite different from those arising when estimates are averaged over a number of years. This is because of the effects of the learning curve, among other things.

2. Costs have an annoying habit of changing through time (usually upwards); The assumption of a fixed selling price and unchanging variable and fixed costs is often not realistic except in the short term.

3. Break-even analysis requires the incorporation of strategies for production and sales and the strategies adopted may have a great influence on the costs incurred. Often the model will be used, as we discussed earlier, to assess alternative strategies with differing break-even points, sales levels and profit results.

4. There are genuine difficulties in separating costs into fixed and variable elements, despite the availability of analysis techniques.

5. There is no consideration given to the effect of the new product on the existing product mix or sales mix. This is particularly serious when the new product either competes for resources with an existing product, or provides resources for other products.

6   The analysis does not indicate the time pattern of sales or expenditures within the period. If all expenditure is to occur before any sales revenue is collected, the situation is quite different from one where the expenditure and sales occur together.

What we have seen is that a combination of cost analysis and cost-of-capital calculations can indicate the sales levels at which budgets should be planned. If all of this looks too difficult, there are computer packages available which will do all of the work for you provided you can calculate the key figures. These computer models are getting better all the time as computers become more sophisticated, but we will know that the computer is really human when it can make a mistake then blame it on another machine.

# 7

# Mapping the Road to Success: Budgeting

Most books on finance make outrageous statements about the absolute necessity for planning everything down to the last dollar. It is true that sensible planning increases the chances of success, but some people get on very well without it. I will never forget Charlie Brancic. I had heard about Charlie through a student of mine who had approached him about making a study of his business systems as a field project. She couldn't believe it and neither could I. Here was a five-million-dollars a-year business supplying components to the motor industry with no systems at all. There was no planning, no budgets, no cash handling system, no analysis, no break-even calculations. Nothing. Thinking that there was a marvelous chance for a major consulting contract I could hardly wait to rush out and see for myself.

'You mean that you don't do any cash planning at all? You just hope for the best. What if you didn't have enough to pay the wages one week?'

'Always I pay the wages.'

'But what if some time you didn't have enough to pay the wages?'

'It never happen.'

'What if you had trouble paying suppliers?'

'No trouble, no time.'

'But all businesses plan for success. Don't you ever have problems in buying things?'

'Last week I have problem.'

'Aha, I knew that would have to happen sometimes. What went wrong?' I had him at last.

'My wife, she come back from holiday in Europe and America and she decide she want Mercedes Sports like mine. I have to tell her wait one week then okay, because I had to pay for new house that week.'

I retreated quietly to my old beaten-up Falcon and sneaked away.

It is not usually like that. Charlie is an exception. **Nearly everybody who doesn't budget will finish up broke.**

The budget is only one part of the planning process. Planning starts with the setting of long-term objectives and long-term planning ahead to achieve them. Then there will be intermediate-term objectives and intermediate-term planning. The budget refers only to the immediate plans for the current periods.

## Long-Term Planning

Long-term planning looks at emerging needs five to ten years ahead. Management will consider emerging trends such as changes in community attitudes which may affect work habits, family life and social conditions. One property-investment trust based in Sydney recognised that the growth in divorce in Australia provided opportunities. It estimated that, as people became divorced, they would share the proceeds from the family home and would be looking for quality apartments with low maintenance requirements situated on the north shore. So they invested in property suitable for this market segment well before other investors picked up the same trend. Their unit-holders made record gains some six or seven years later.

Another important long-term factor is changes in economic conditions which may influence the disposable income of consumers or influence wealth distribution. International, as well as local conditions should be considered.

A few years ago when the OPEC nations forced up the oil price, there was a general belief that petrol prices would become very high and consumers would want motor cars with smaller engines and lower fuel consumption. Hence plans were made to produce smaller motor cars in Australia. For a number of reasons the petrol price rise has not been as dramatic as was expected and the trend to smaller cars has not been as sudden as was anticipated. This has caused Ford, which planned to stay with its 'family Six' size Falcon despite the predictions, to overtake its competitors who went for smaller cars.

One problem with long-term planning is that you won't always be right, and being wrong can be very costly. Changes in technology have been taking place at an accelerating rate. Whole industries exist today which rely on technology which was unknown even ten years ago. Picking a winner and riding it to success can lead to very rapid expansion of a business. When the first computers appeared, some experts believed that there would never be a need for more than six of them in the world. They were certain that there was no chance of developing a computer industry. Others with more vision set about building an industry.

A prominent industrialist watching the Wright Brothers fly said that the invention had no application to passenger traffic as it was too windy and dangerous sitting on the wings. Others were planning commercial applications of aviation even at that stage. When Melbourne was planned, with its wide streets, experts said that it was a waste of land because if you had enough horses to fill the streets you would never be able to dispose of all of the horse manure.

Changes in political and legal conditions can be important for long-term business planning. Changes in taxation laws may open up or close whole areas of investment. Changing government attitudes to working hours, restraint of trade, human rights and provision of services can create opportunities. At the moment in Australia we see a shortage of government-funded facilities for tertiary education. This has led to the emergence of our first privately-owned university. A closing door for one person is an opportunity for another.

The population structure is another factor to watch. As the birth-rate has dropped in Australia and the 'post-war babies' have aged, we have a much older population than in the past. Provision of accommodation, medical services and leisure activities for people over forty years of age has become a boom industry. Many of the biggest businesses in this field anticipated the development a decade ago and planned for the spectacular growth that they have achieved.

So, careful long-term planning which takes into consideration the emerging trends can lead to spectacular business growth for those who get it right and disaster for those who ignore it or get it wrong. Obviously it is very difficult to conduct long-range planning with the precision in numbers expected of short-term budgeting. Most long-range plans may not be quantified at all except in the broadest terms. However, they will define the direction to be taken in the intermediate-term plans.

## Intermediate-Term Planning

At the intermediate-term planning stage it becomes more important to start putting numbers on the projections. It may become necessary to answer questions like:

1   How much will pollution control cost us? Is there a cheaper way of doing it?

2   Will the raw materials we need be available? How much are they likely to cost?

3   How will the public react to our product? Will there be sufficient demand for it or will we need to stimulate, or even create, a demand?

4   What are our competitors likely to be doing? Will we be a market leader or a follower? Should we try to avoid head-to-head competition?

5   What will energy prices be like? Are there cheaper, more efficient sources of energy?

6   Will we maintain or increase market share? Do we need to take any special steps to ensure that we do so?

7   Can our existing management cope? Do we need more managers or can the skills be developed in existing management?

8   What research and development is necessary? Will we do this ourselves or buy knowledge or rights to processes developed elsewhere?

9   Do we have the required production capacity? Must we build more plants? Extend existing facilities? Take on and train more employees? Investigate the use of robots?

10  Where will we get the money for all of this? Will we borrow, or make more share issues? Will we pay low dividends and retain most of the profits for development purposes?

Out of the answers to these and similar questions will come more definite planning and the numbers will be more specific as the plans come closer to fulfillment. The intermediate-term objectives will provide targets in the operating plans for the year after the current budget, and as the numbers become firm they will set the parameters of that year's budget so that the budget figures themselves become negotiable only within that framework. Any discussion of the budget estimates will be limited to a range of possibilities consistent with the figures which emerge from the intermediate-term objectives.

## Annual Budgets

Budgets have two distinct purposes which are of equal importance. These are **planning** and **control**. The budget represents a plan, usually in monetary terms, of what is to be attempted in the current period. It also acts as a guide to what should be happening as the year progresses. As long as the budgeted revenues are made and expenses are kept within the budget limits then the budgeted profit figure must be achieved.

In order to make it easier to keep a careful check on the progress of the business, budgets are usually prepared for the whole year, then divided into shorter time periods such as quarters, months, weeks or even days. Some parts of the budget may not be set in dollar amounts. Production budgets in a paper mill for instance, may be set as a certain tonnage per day as this is more meaningful to the people involved than a dollar sum.

For a budget to work properly, the people using it must have a commitment to it. If the budget is created by a separate group of planners, then imposed on the people using it, the users may lack commitment to it. The level of commitment can often be increased dramatically by involving people in the budget's preparation. Therefore participatory budgeting, with all people in management positions being involved, has become very popular. This usually means that figures are sought from departments within the organisation and these are passed on up the management line. When they prove unsatisfactory to higher management, they come back again for revision. No amount of budget participation by lower-level management will change the overall figures to any great extent. As we have seen, the overall pattern has been set through the intermediate-term planning. This annual budgeting scramble is mainly about slicing up the cake rather than the size of the cake.

Budgeting is not fully effective unless the budget is accepted by the lower levels of management. This acceptance will depend upon the attitude of higher management and the way in which budget information is used. Any indication given by top management that it does not fully support the budget or budgeting in general will have a devastating effect on its acceptance at lower levels. Preparing a budget is not easy work and if top management is not enthusiastic about it, then it is unlikely that anybody else will be.

The budget should not be used as a pressure device to attribute blame for problems which arise. The aim should be to use the budget in setting goals, measuring results and identifying areas requiring attention. The users should see the budget as an aid to the achievement of both individual and company goals.

Too often accountants become preoccupied with the numbers in the budget and lose sight of the human motivation aspects. Where you are faced with this type of situation you should discuss the matter calmly with the offending accountant. Full

confrontation will be counter-productive, particularly as that type of accountant is likely to feel threatened by what are seen as attacks on the accountant's domain. A quiet discussion about what you see as the most important points of the situation, with an assurance that the matter is not out of control is at least worth a try.

## The Master Budget

The master budget is a network of interdependent budgets covering various aspects of the budget process. It is the major control instrument for the next period's activities. Figure 7.1 shows the interrelationship of the various components of the master budget.

## Figure 7.1  The Master Budget

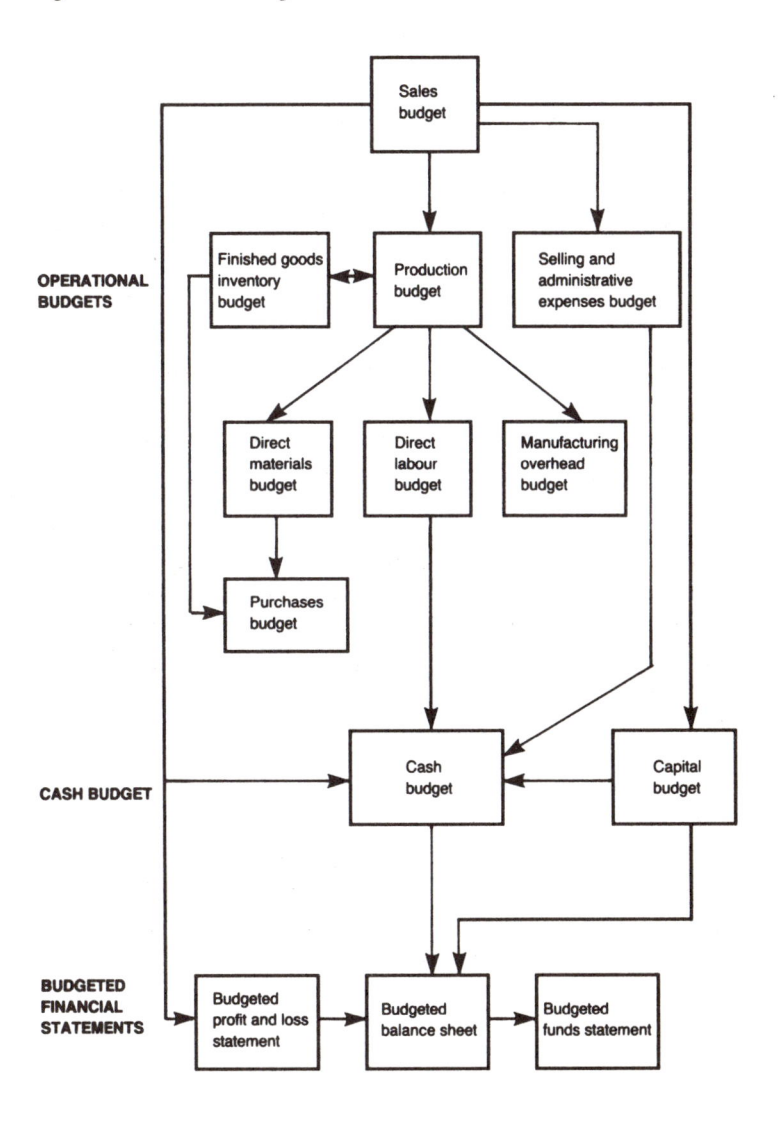

**OPERATIONAL BUDGETS**

**CASH BUDGET**

**BUDGETED FINANCIAL STATEMENTS**

The overall framework of the master budget contains three major components:

1. The operational budgets. These are used to project the revenue and expenses involved in the operations of the business, which, of course, will have an important influence on both profit and cashflow.

2. The cash budget. This budget is of critical importance as it helps to ensure a satisfactory cash situation throughout the period.

3. The budgeted financial statements. These are a budgeted profit and loss statement, budgeted balance sheet and budgeted funds statement. They are projections of how these statements will appear at the next balance date if the budget is followed exactly.

We shall begin with the operational budgets. We shall assume that the master budget is for the next year. However, some parts of it may be subdivided into shorter periods.

## The Sales Budget

The whole budget structure relies on the sales budget. As was indicated in chapter 5, this may be prepared using macroforecasting, microforecasting or a combination of both. The sales budget will show the expected sales for the next period in both units and dollars. Since the sales levels will affect all other projections, it is extremely important that sales estimates be accurate. The sales budget may be subdivided into sales territories, and shorter time periods such as quarters, seasons, months or weeks. The sales budget in Figure 7.2 is for Terry's Tables Ltd. As you can see, it has been prepared on a quarterly basis. The company's only product is a wooden wine table. Sales peak in the second quarter of the financial year, due to Christmas. All sales are made for cash.

**Figure 7.2**
**TERRY'S TABLES LTD**
Sales Budget (Schedule 1) for the year ended 30 June 19--

|  | Quarter 1 | Quarter 2 | Quarter 3 | Quarter 4 | Year |
|---|---|---|---|---|---|
| Expected sales (units) | 1 600 | 2 200 | 900 | 1 300 | 6 000 |
| Selling price (per unit) | $200 | 200 | 200 | 200 | 200 |
|  | $320 000 | $440 000 | $180 000 | $260 000 | $1 200 000 |

## The Production Budget

The next step is to work out how many tables we need to produce to give us the product to sell. So we will prepare a production budget. This budget uses the existing levels of inventory, the projected sales shown in the sales budget, and the desired minimum level of inventory, to establish how many units of the product Terry's Tables will need to produce to maintain acceptable inventory levels. The outline of this budget, which could be set out in any one of a variety of formats, will show that:

minimum desired level of inventory at the end of the period

    **plus** projected sales (from the sales budget)

    **equals** total units required during the period

    **less** inventory on hand at the start of the period

    **equals** production required during the period.

We can now construct the production budget for Terry's Tables Ltd (Figure 7.3). Firms usually set their desired inventory according to the requirements of the following month or quarter. We will assume here that Terry's Tables Ltd requires an inventory at the end of a period equal to 20 per cent of the next quarter's sales. The sales figures come from the sales budget, the beginning inventory from last year's balance sheet.

**Figure 7.3**
**TERRY'S TABLES LTD**
Production Budget (Schedule 2) for the year ended 30 June 19--

|  | Quarter |  |  |  | Year |
|---|---|---|---|---|---|
|  | 1 | 2 | 3 | 4 |  |
| Expected sales (units) | 1 600 | 2 200 | 900 | 1 300 | 6 000 |
| Add: Desired ending inventory | 440 | 180 | 260 | 320 | 320 |
| TOTAL NEEDS | 2 040 | 2 380 | 1 160 | 1 620 | 6 320 |
| Less: Beginning inventory | 320 | 440 | 180 | 260 | 320 |
| Units to be produced | 1 720 | 1 940 | 980 | 1 360 | 6 000 |

Now that we know how many tables we are going to schedule for production, we can work out our requirements for raw material and labour. A purchase budget is only used where the business purchases finished goods. Some manufacturing companies may do this as well as producing their own goods, while trading businesses may operate by buying and selling goods without manufacturing at all. The basis of calculation in the purchases budget is the same as that used in the production budget except that the bottom line is the number of units that must be purchased during the time period. If there are a number of different items traded, the budget calculation must be made for each one separately.

## The Direct Materials Budget

The next budget, for Terry's Tables, the direct materials budget, is sometimes incorporated as part of a cost of production budget. The aim of the direct materials budget is to calculate the quantity and cost of raw materials required for the period. It is set out in the same way as the production and purchases budgets. The calculations must be made for all raw materials used. The quantity of materials required will depend largely upon the production level which was calculated in the production budget. Terry's Tables Ltd has always tried to keep material inventories of 25 per cent of the next quarter's requirements. Figure 7.4 shows the calculations for the amount of timber needed.

**Figure 7.4**
**TERRY'S TABLES LTD**
**Direct Materials Budget (Schedule 3) for the year ended 30 June 19--**

|  | Quarter |  |  |  | Year |
|---|---|---|---|---|---|
|  | 1 | 2 | 3 | 4 |  |
| Units to be produced (from production budget) | 1 720 | 1 940 | 980 | 1 360 | 6 000 |
| Timber required per unit (linear metres) | 6 | 6 | 6 | 6 | 6 |
| PRODUCTION NEEDS (metres) | 10 320 | 11 640 | 5 880 | 8 160 | 36 000 |
| Add: Desired inventory at end of quarter (metres) | 2 910 | 1 470 | 2 040 | 2 580 | 2 580 |
| TOTAL NEEDS (metres) | 13 230 | 13 110 | 7 920 | 10 740 | 38 580 |
| Less: Beginning inventory | 2 580 | 2 910 | 1 470 | 2 040 | 2 580 |
| RAW MATERIAL TO BE PURCHASED (metres) | 10 650 | 10 200 | 6 450 | 8 700 | 36 000 |
| Cost per metre | $2 | 2 | 2 | 2 | 2 |
| COST OF RAW MATERIALS TO BE PURCHASED | $21 300 | $20 400 | $12 900 | $17 400 | $72 000 |

## The Direct Labour Budget

The direct labour budget is also developed from the information calculated in the production budget. It will enable the business to estimate not only the labour costs but the quantity of each type of labour required. This allows the company to adjust labour levels in advance and so avoid shortages of labour at critical times. It also reduces the likelihood of having to suddenly retrench labour. Erratic hiring and firing of staff reduces morale and leads to insecurity, inefficiency and industrial disputes. Engineering studies will determine the number of labour hours required per unit and from this the total labour requirements can be calculated. Of course, if more than one type of labour is required, separate calculations must be made for each. In this case all labour involved is of the same type (see Figure 7.5).

Figure 7.5
TERRY'S TABLES LTD
Direct Labour Budget (Schedule 4) for the year ended 30 June 19--

|  | Quarter 1 | Quarter 2 | Quarter 3 | Quarter 4 | Year |
|---|---|---|---|---|---|
| Units to be produced (from production budget) | 1 720 | 1 940 | 980 | 1 360 | 6 000 |
| Direct labour hours required per unit | 2.5 | 2.5 | 2.5 | 2.5 | 2.5 |
| TOTAL LABOUR HOURS REQUIRED | 4 300 | 4 850 | 2 450 | 3 400 | 15 000 |
| Direct labour cost per hour | $9 | 9 | 9 | 9 | 9 |
| TOTAL DIRECT LABOUR COST | $38 700 | $43 650 | $22 050 | $30 600 | $135 000 |

## The Manufacturing Overheads Budget

Having calculated the cost of raw materials and direct labour we must now consider overheads. This brings us to the manufacturing overhead budget. In manufacturing operations there are many overhead costs beyond the direct costs of raw materials and factory labour. These overheads cover such things as energy costs for production, heating and lighting, insurance, rates and rent, lease of equipment, management salaries and maintenance. Each of these costs has its own particular pattern of behavior, so estimates must be made separately for them. From all of this information, an overhead rate can be calculated on some convenient basis such as direct labour hours.

We saw in chapter 5 that costs can be either fixed or variable, so separate figures are developed for fixed and variable overheads. Terry's Tables Ltd has calculated that for the coming year variable overheads will cost $4 per direct labour hour worked and fixed costs are $140,000 for the year (see Figure 7.6). Depreciation will be subtracted for purposes of the cash budget because it is an expense not requiring the payment of any cash.

**Figure 7.6**
**TERRY'S TABLES LTD**
**Manufacturing Overhead Budget (Schedule 5) for the year ended 30 June 19--**

|  | Quarter 1 | Quarter 2 | Quarter 3 | Quarter 4 | Year |
|---|---|---|---|---|---|
| Budgeted direct labour hours | 4 300 | 4 850 | 2 450 | 3 400 | 15 000 |
| Variable overhead rate (per hour) | $4 | 4 | 4 | 4 | 4 |
| Budgeted variable overhead | 17 200 | 19 400 | 9 800 | 13 600 | 60 000 |
| Budgeted fixed overhead | 35 000 | 35 000 | 35 000 | 35 000 | 140 000 |
| Total budgeted overheads | 52 200 | 54 400 | 44 800 | 48 600 | 200 000 |
| Less: Depreciation | 4 000 | 4 000 | 4 000 | 4 000 | 16 000 |
| CASH DISBURSEMENTS FOR OVERHEAD | $48 200 | $50 400 | $40 800 | $44 600 | $184 000 |

## The Finished Goods Inventory Budget

At this stage it is possible to calculate the cost of a unit of production, whether it be a chair, a liter of wine, a tonne of aluminium ingots or a cubic meter of timber. It is important to make this calculation so that it can be used in setting prices and valuing the finished goods inventory. The details are set out in the finished goods inventory budget (Figure 7.7).

**Figure 7.7**
**TERRY'S TABLES LTD**
**Finished Goods Inventory Budget (Schedule 6) for the year ended 30 June 19--**

| Item | Quantity | Cost | Total |
|---|---|---|---|
| Cost per unit: | | | |
| Direct materials | 6 metres | $2 per metre | $12.00 |
| Direct Labour | 2.5 hours | $9 per hour | 22.50 |
| Manufacturing overhead | | | |
| Cost per unit | 2.5 hours | $13.33 per hour* | 33.33 |
| | | | $67.83 |
| Budgeted finished goods inventory: | | | |
| 320 units at $67.83 per unit | = $21 706 | | |

*Total budgeted overheads ($200 000) ÷ total budgeted direct labour hours (15 000).

## The Selling and Administrative Expenses Budget

Once the goods are manufactured, that is not the end of the expenses. Selling expenses will be incurred in promotion and advertising, marketing administration, salesmen's salaries, commissions and expenses, delivery and storage. Administration expenses apply to the whole business, covering items like office wages, management salaries, computer costs, depreciation on office equipment, insurance and accounting (which is very important). For Terry's Tables Ltd, these are set out in the selling and administrative expenses budget (Figure 7.8).

**Figure 7.8**
**TERRY'S TABLES LTD**
**Selling and Administrative Expenses Budget (Schedule 7) for the year ended 30 June 19--**

|  | Quarter 1 | Quarter 2 | Quarter 3 | Quarter 4 | Year |
|---|---|---|---|---|---|
| Budgeted sales (units) | 1 600 | 2 200 | 900 | 1 300 | 6 000 |
| Variable selling and administrative expense (per unit) | $3 | 3 | 3 | 3 | 3 |
| BUDGETED VARIABLE EXPENSE | $4 800 | $6 600 | $2 700 | $3 900 | $18 000 |
| Fixed selling and administrative expenses |  |  |  |  |  |
| Advertising | 5 000 | 3 000 | 2 000 | 2 000 | 12 000 |
| Management salaries | 65 000 | 65 000 | 65 000 | 65 000 | 260 000 |
| Insurance | — | 6 200 | — | — | 6 200 |
| Rent | 6 000 | 6 000 | 6 000 | 6 000 | 24 000 |
| Salesmen's salaries | 44 000 | 44 000 | 44 000 | 44 000 | 176 000 |
| TOTAL BUDGETED SELLING AND ADMINISTRATIVE EXPENSES | $124 800 | $130 800 | $119 700 | $120 900 | $496 200 |

The last of the operational budgets is the capital budget, which covers major items of equipment, new buildings and plants, takeovers and major investments. Chapter 10 is devoted to the special techniques used in this area.

## The Cash Budget

The second major component of the master budget is the cash budget. This is designed to show the cash receipts and disbursements of cash that should occur. When these are combined with the opening cash balance and desired minimum cash levels, the surplus or deficiency in cash can be computed. If a deficiency is expected, management can arrange financing in advance. It is a lot more impressive handing the bank manager a cash budget and saying 'It looks like we may have a deficiency in October and November, will you be able to help us out?', than having to ring up in desperation when you realise that you are sliding into overdraft. The cash budget has four major sections:

1   Receipts - the cash inflows expected.
2   Disbursements - the cash outflows expected.
3   Excess or deficiency - section 1 minus section 2.
4   Financing - How to solve problems in section 3.

The cash budget will be broken down into time periods that are as short as is feasible. A quarterly breakdown is likely to be very misleading and even a monthly breakdown may be too long. Many firms calculate cash budgets on a weekly basis. In large companies a daily cash budget basis is often used. When I worked in a large manufacturing company we calculated our budgeted cash balance for each day, about a week ahead. This enabled us to place surpluses on the short-term money market so that no money was left unused in bank accounts. This earned the company thousands of dollars every year.

The main restraint on detailed budgeting of this kind is the cost. Clearly, the more detail you put into budgeting the greater the resources required to prepare the budgets and the higher the cost. Smaller firms often find that monthly cash budgets are sufficient. In some cases firms have discovered that the low point in their cash balance occurs at about the twenty-first day of the month, when bills have been paid but customers' payments are still coming in. This may lead them to calculate monthly cash balances as at the twenty-first of each month, rather than the last day of the month, so that they are not misled. In this instance, to simplify the calculations, we will assume that Terry's Tables Ltd prepares its cash budget on a quarterly basis. The company requires a minimum cash balance of $10 000 (see Figure 7.9).

**Figure 7.9**
**TERRY'S TABLES LTD**
Cash Budget (Schedule 8) for the year ended 30 June 19--

|  | Schedule | Quarter 1 | Quarter 2 | Quarter 3 | Quarter 4 | Year |
|---|---|---|---|---|---|---|
| Cash balance at beginning |  | $14 000 | 33 000 | 10 000 | 10 000 | 14 000 |
| Add: Receipts: |  |  |  |  |  |  |
| Sales | 1 | 320 000 | 440 000 | 180 000 | 260 000 | 1 200 000 |
| TOTAL CASH AVAILABLE |  | $334 000 | $473 000 | $190 000 | $270 000 | $1 214 000 |
| Less: Disbursements |  |  |  |  |  |  |
| Direct materials | 3 | 21 300 | 20 400 | 12 900 | 17 400 | 72 000 |
| Direct labour | 4 | 38 700 | 43 650 | 22 050 | 30 600 | 135 000 |
| Manufacturing overhead | 5 | 48 200 | 50 400 | 40 800 | 44 600 | 184 000 |
| Selling and admin. | 7 | 124 800 | 130 800 | 119 700 | 120 900 | 496 200 |
| Income taxes | 9 | 40 000 | 40 000 |  | 40 000 | 120 000 |
| Equipment purchases |  |  | 200 000 |  |  | 200 000 |
| Dividends | 9 |  | 40 000 |  |  | 40 000 |
| TOTAL DISBURSEMENTS |  | $273 000 | $525 250 | $195 450 | $253 500 | $1 247 200 |
| Excess (deficiency) of cash available |  | 61 000 | (52 250) | (5 450) | 16 500 | 19 800 |
| Financing: |  |  |  |  |  |  |
| Borrowings (at beginning) |  | 28 000 | — | 62 250 | 77 700 | 28 000 |
| New borrowings (repayments) |  | (28 000) | 62 250 | 15 450 | (6 500) | 71 200 |
| CASH BALANCE, ENDING |  | $33 000 | $10 000 | $10 000 | $10 000 | $10 000 |

It may be as well to reconcile the figures in the cash budget, particularly in the financing section. Taken over the whole year the company will have disbursements of $33,200 more than cash available. It will also repay the $28,000 owing at the start of the year and keep a further $10,000 as a minimum acceptable cash balance. Hence, at the end of the year it will owe $33,200 plus $28,000 plus $10,000, equaling $71,200, which is the net figure on the borrowings (repayments) line.

Of course, if the management does not like the thought of owing this sum at the end of the year, the budget must be adjusted and reworked. Perhaps the equipment intended for purchase in the second quarter could be leased instead. This would solve all cash flow problems and remove the need for any borrowings.

## The Budgeted Financial Statements

The final component of the master budget is the budgeted financial statements. These budgeted statements will be based on the information contained in the operational budgets and the cash budget. They are for internal purposes, and the format is the same as that for the external statements produced at the end of a period.

The budgeted profit and loss statement or revenue statement (see Figure 7.10) contains the revenue and expenses classified into meaningful categories. These categories will vary according to the type of business but a common basis used is to classify them according to cost of goods sold, selling expenses, administrative expenses and financial expenses.

## The Budgeted Balance Sheet and Budgeted Funds Statement

The last two elements of the master budget are the budgeted balance sheet (Figure 7.11) and the budgeted funds statement (Figure 7.12). The budgeted balance sheet is based on the current balance sheet with the numbers being adjusted according to the information in the other parts of the master budget.

**Figure 7.10**
**TERRY'S TABLES LTD**
**Budgeted Profit and Loss Statement (Schedule 9) for the year ended 30 June 19--**

|  | Schedule |  |
|---|---|---|
| Sales (6 000 units at $200) | 1 | $1 200 000 |
| Less: Cost of goods sold (6 000 units at $67.83) | 6 | 406 980 |
| GROSS PROFIT |  | 793 020 |
| Less: Selling and administrative expenses |  | 496 200 |
| NET OPERATING PROFIT BEFORE TAX |  | 296 820 |
| Less: Income tax |  | 120 000 |
| OPERATING PROFIT |  | 176 820 |
| Current retained earnings |  | 18 856 |
| Available for appropriation |  | 195 676 |
| Less: Proposed dividends |  | 40 000 |
| PROPOSED RETAINED EARNINGS |  | $155 676 |

The figures for Plant and equipment, accumulated depreciation, land and paid-up capital are taken from the balance sheet with the additional depreciation allowed for in the budget calculations.

The budgeted funds statement was prepared by comparing the budgeted balance sheet with the existing current balance sheet and listing the changes. If management do not approve of the effects that the funds statement shows, they can adjust them by altering the budget to get a different result. This may be done several times before an acceptable result emerges.

**Figure 7.11**
**TERRY'S TABLES LTD**
**Budgeted Balance Sheet as at 30 June 19--**

| | | |
|---|---:|---:|
| *ASSETS* | | |
| *Current assets* | | |
|   Cash | $10 000 | |
|   Raw materials stocks | 5 160 | |
|   Finished goods stocks | 21 706 | $36 866 |
| *Non-current assets* | | |
|   Plant and equipment | 340 010* | |
|   Less: Accumulated depreciation | 100 000* | |
| | 240 010 | |
|   Land | 200 000* | 440 010 |
| **TOTAL ASSETS** | | **$476 876** |
| *Current liabilities* | | |
|   Bank loan | | 71 200 |
| *Shareholders' funds* | | |
|   Paid-up capital | 250 000* | |
|   Retained earnings | 155 676 | 405 676 |
| **TOTAL EQUITIES** | | **$476 876** |

*These figures are taken from the current balance sheet with the additional depreciation written off in the budget calculations.

## Zero Base Budgeting

A comparatively recent development which began in the American Defense Department is zero base budgeting. This gets its name from the requirement that managers must justify all costs regardless of the past situation; all costs must be justified as if everything is a new project. One major requirement is that each department rank its activities in order of priority from 'essential' down to 'optional'. This is done every year so no costs are regarded as ongoing from year to year. The main objection to the technique is that it can become akin to 'reinventing the wheel' every year with consequent inefficiencies in the use of resources. The costs incurred in doing it may be greater than the savings made.

**Figure 7.12**
**TERRY'S TABLES LTD**
**Budgeted Funds Statement for the year ended 30 June 19--**

| | | |
|---|---|---|
| Funds were provided by: | | |
| 1 Funds from trading: | | |
| Revenue | $1 200 000 | |
| Less: Expenses requiring funds | 1 007 180 | |
| FUNDS FROM TRADING | | $192 820 |
| 2 Decrease in assets | | |
| Land | | 20 000 |
| 3 Increase in liability | | |
| Bank loan | | 43 200 |
| TOTAL FUNDS PROVIDED | | $256 020 |
| Funds were applied as follows: | | |
| 1 Increases in assets | | |
| Equipment* | | 216 020 |
| 2 Payment of dividend | | 40 000 |
| TOTAL FUNDS APPLIED | | $256 020 |

*This represents the equipment purchased for cash, plus a small credit purchase of equipment.

## The Budget as a Control Mechanism

Once the budget is set, its role as a planning procedure is finished. It then begins to act as a control device. A large amount of time and effort will have gone into preparing the budget and we must presume that the achievement of the budgeted figures will be a satisfactory result. If it wasn't we would be working to a different set of figures. So, provided everything is 'on budget', all is well, but variances from budget are investigated closely. This type of approach is referred to as management by exception.

## Management by Exception

Management by exception is quite a natural approach. We do it all the time in our everyday lives. When you get up each morning you don't go off to the doctor for a full medical inspection to see if you'll make it through the day. You only go when something appears to be wrong. You don't strip your car engine down every morning to see if the bearings are still all right; you assume they are until a rattle develops. Management by exception is the same approach. We only investigate if serious variances from budget exist.

## Responsibility Accounting

Modern organisation most commonly use responsibility accounting. This recognises that anybody who has control over cost or revenue is a responsibility centre. Effectively, this means that if you are responsible for some cost or revenue item and therefore have been involved in setting the budget, your actual performance is then measured and the two are compared. As a manager, no matter how far down the line, you will receive a performance report which points out the variances between budget and actual performance in your area of responsibility.

## Performance Reports

A performance report can be set up in many different ways. Suppose, for example, that the Burple Company Ltd has budgeted to produce 100 000 burples during November. The plant manager has a budget (Figure 7.13) which shows the overhead expenses that he controls. We will assume that because of industrial disputes only 80 000 burples were produced in November, and the actual overhead expenses were indirect materials $67 000, lubricants $3 300 and power $17 400. A performance report might be prepared to show the results (Figure 7.14). Notice variances are regarded as favourable (F) if they would increase profit, unfavorable (U) if they would reduce profit.

**Figure 7.13**
**BURPLE COMPANY LTD**
**Plant Manager's Budget for month of November 19--**

| | |
|---|---:|
| *Budgeted production in units* | 100 000 |
| *Budgeted overheads* | |
| Indirect materials | $80 000 |
| Lubricants | 4 000 |
| Power | 20 000 |
| TOTAL | $104 000 |

**Figure 7.14**
**BURPLE COMPANY LTD**
**Budget Performance Report for month of November 19--**

| | *Actual* | *Budget* | *Variance* |
|---|---:|---:|---:|
| *Production in units* | 80 000 | 100 000 | 20 000 U |
| *Overhead costs* | | | |
| Indirect materials | $67 000 | 80 000 | 13 000 F |
| Lubricants | 3 300 | 4 000 | 700 F |
| Power | 17 400 | 20 000 | 2 600 F |
| | $87 700 | $104 000 | $16 300 F |

This report appears, on the face of it, to indicate that performance in this plant has been very good and that overhead costs are $16 300 lower than expected. But is it really that good?

Remember production is only 80 per cent of what was expected, and aren't all of those cost variable costs? Surely the variable costs should also only be 80 per cent of the budgeted levels. They are, in fact, 84 per cent.

So performance reports can be misleading unless allowances are made for the type of costs involved. The way to overcome this situation is to use flexible budgeting for variable costs. So far we have assumed that the budget is static. That is, the budget sets down the same figures regardless of the level of production. As we just saw with the Burple Company Ltd this can be dangerously misleading. The costs in that case are all variable costs so why not express them according to a 'per unit' basis then calculate the budget figure according to the actual production level achieved. This is what a flexible budget does.

## Flexible Budgets

If we look more closely at the Burple Company's budget for overheads we can see that the figures given were set assuming production of 100 000 units. If those expenses are fully variable, they represent costs per unit as follows:

Indirect materials, 80 cents;

Lubricants, 4 cents;

Power, 20 cents.

A flexible budget will produce a performance report which is calculated on that basis. So when the Burple Company Ltd produces only 80 000 units with the actual costs for November which were given earlier, the performance report would appear as in Figure 7.15.

**Figure 7.15**
**BURPLE COMPANY LTD**
Performance Report for November 19-- (flexible budget)

|  |  | Actual | Budget | Variance |
|---|---|---|---|---|
| Production in units |  | 80 000 | 100 000 | 20 000 U |
| Overhead costs | Unit rate |  |  |  |
| Indirect materials | 0.80 | $67 000 | 64 000 | 3 000 U |
| Lubricants | 0.04 | 3 300 | 3 200 | 100 U |
| Power | 0.20 | 17 400 | 16 000 | 1 400 U |
|  |  | $87 700 | $83 200 | $4 500 U |

As you can see, this picture is completely different from that given by the static budget we used earlier. Because it takes into consideration the actual production level achieved, the flexible budget gives the manager more meaningful information. These days, nearly all manufacturing businesses use flexible budgeting for variable costs. As a manager, you want the best possible information so that you always know just exactly what position you are in. Knowing your position is always very important.

There was a raging storm and the coastguard patrol was picking up weak signals from a small yacht many kilometers out to sea.

'Mayday, mayday,' the radio crackled. 'This is the yacht Gladiator. We're taking water in a bad way. I think we're about to go down.'

'How many aboard?'

'There're just the three of us. Please help us. The radio's failing and the water's rising.'

'What is your position? What is your position?'

There was silence. Then the crackling message:

'Well I can't exactly see why it matters but I'm the production manager of a small computer software company.'

# 8

# Working Capital Management

When we talk about the 'working capital' we're certainly not talking about Canberra. Nobody works in Canberra. Working capital is the funds used by business in its everyday activities, and just because a business is doing well it does not mean that working capital can be left to look after itself.

It's a sad world.

Your great-aunt Mildred has just died and you know that you're going to get $80 000 from her will. Your bonus is due next month, the $3 000 you've toiled, suffered, hauled and crawled for. You know that you could borrow a couple of grand from your girlfriend but she's up on the Gold Coast. Potentially you've got packets but at the moment things are a little tight. You don't have enough for a bus fare. You've no working capital and you can't do the things that you want to do. If it makes you feel any better, you are not alone. Businesses often have the same problem.

## Working Capital

In a business the working capital consists of the balance between current assets and current liabilities. Working capital management is, then, the management of the current assets and current liabilities. Anything that affects either a current asset or a current liability affects the working capital. In managing the working capital there are three major tasks:

1   making sure that the level of current assets maximises the firm's profitability;

2   making sure that there is the best possible balance between long-term and short-term debt, to keep the average cost of capital as low as possible;

3   making sure that funds are not squandered by keeping assets that are not productive.

## Ensuring the Business Has the Right Composition of Assets

A good starting point in achieving these important goals is to make sure that the firm has the right composition of assets. This usually involves the consideration of 'trade-offs' between various ways of doing things. For instance, if a firm decides to invest heavily in automated equipment it will save on the need for human resources. If it invests in its own delivery vehicles, it will save in payments to outside contractors. Let us consider some of the major resources in a firm and their implications for resource planning.

## Labour as an Asset

Labour does not appear in the balance sheet as an asset, but in many firms it is the most important resource. Take an advertising agency for example. All of its equipment, office machinery, debtors and stocks of materials appear in its balance sheet. However, its most valuable asset - the creative people who work there - doesn't. Why?

It's a practical problem of valuation. As you've seen already, accountants favour valuing assets at their cost. What is the cost of a creative person? Two approaches have been tried to work this out. The first is to take the initial cost of hiring the person: the advertisement, employment agency fee, cost of time used in interviewing and cost of correspondence. Add to this the cost of training, formal and informal and perhaps the cost of the time used by other people in that process. But how do you know how much of other people's time has gone into that training? Some people learn quickly, others we'd rather not talk about. Even if we can assess all of this with something approaching accuracy, the figure we will get bears no relationship to the person's ongoing value to the firm. For the average creative person (if such exists) this might be about $8 000.

The alternative approach is to value people according to what they are paid. If a person is paid $35 000 a year that is their value as an asset. But why not value them at two years' salary? Or three years? It is very arbitrary. You and I both know people who get a lot more than we do, who are worth a lot less to the firm than we are.

So valuing your labour force is a very difficult task and accountants have responded to this difficulty by putting it in the too hard basket and not valuing them at all. But that does not mean that they have no value. Many firms succeed or fail because of the availability of a skilled, motivated labour force. Some even locate in a certain area to be close to this resource. If there is a shortage of the right kind of labour, the company may recruit workers and train them. Another possibility is to automate the process. This would mean substituting equipment for labour. If you do this, though, you'll create the need for other workers such as maintenance technicians and operators. You will also increase your operating leverage. Operating leverage refers to the extent to which fixed costs are used in the organisation. With high fixed costs relative to variable costs, profits are much more sensitive to changes in sales. A small increase in sales can cause a substantial increase in profits.

In trying to overcome seasonal variations in demand, some firms treat their employees as temporarily expendable by standing down workers at low periods. This is costly in terms of training effort spent on those workers, and worker morale and productivity in general. Another approach is to keep the same number of employees and build inventory at times of low demand. However, the 'trade-off' is higher inventory costs for storage and financing.

## Managing Cash as an Asset

Cash is, of course, an important resource. If we knew exactly when all of our customers were going to pay, and exactly when we would be required to make all payments, there would be no need to keep any cash at all. We could arrange borrowings to cover times when money would be short and use all cash at the moment it came in. But we don't live in this type of ideal world. A cash balance is necessary because some customers will be late in paying. We may suddenly need to buy an item not planned for. As we saw in chapter 7, the cash budget is the main way of planning cash flow. Do not lose sight of the fact that all assets have to be financed, and the average cost of financing is the weighted average cost of capital for that firm.

If you choose to leave large amounts of cash in the bank, it is costing the same rate to finance as any other asset. As we saw earlier, this may be something approaching 20 per cent per annum. And what is the bank paying you for this act of generosity towards them? Probably nothing, or some near equivalent. Money in business trading accounts is almost entirely unproductive. Therefore, the balance needs to be kept as low as possible.

## Managing Debtors

Debtors is another unproductive asset. Debtors do not pay interest on their debts unless a court judgment has been made against them. All they do is lie there and cost you money to try and collect. Evidence shows that the longer money is owed the harder it will be to collect. At the time of sale you have a 97 per cent chance of collecting the debt. Once it has been owed for three months you have a 70 per cent chance. After six months your chances are less than 50 per cent. All of this time, of course, the cost of financing goes on at the same old rate. If your average cost of capital is 18 per cent and you have an average of $1 million worth of debtors, it will cost you $180 000 for the year to finance those debtors.

Well, if they're so much trouble and they cost so much, why do you have them? Why do you sell on credit at all? The answer is that if you don't you may not make many sales. Selling on credit is a marketing tool. If you don't allow your customers thirty days or maybe more to pay and your competitors will, then your sales will drop, even if your prices are a little lower. So you're stuck with it. However, you must be careful. We all know that maintaining and building market share is of critical importance. But if that means significantly extending the debtors figure, there can be financing problems.

This is particularly the case where, in order to expand your range of customers, you take on some whose credit worthiness is a little suspect. The sales people badly need these new customers to expand sales, but they're in conflict with the credit manager and his allies in accounting. This is one of the classic sources of internal conflict and both groups are likely to be unreasonable. There is no easy answer to the problem, but in an ambitious undertaking, such as the expansion of market share, the chance may have to be taken.

## Managing Stocks

Depending upon the type of business, the firm may have stocks of raw materials, work-in-process and finished goods. The level of finished goods stocks depends largely upon the rate at which sales are made and how long it takes to replace the stock. If customer demand is erratic, higher stock levels are required. Similarly the need to import from overseas will lead to keeping higher stocks.

Work-in-process is the stock that is partially finished in the manufacturing process. The amount of work-in-process depends largely upon the length and complexity of the manufacturing processes and the size of the undertaking. In large complex situations like motor-car assembly lines, the work-in-process can run into many millions of dollars.

Raw materials may be either elemental materials such as iron ore or logs of timber or they may be sophisticated sub-assemblies like silicon chips or gearboxes. The level of raw materials stocks is tied to the production levels, difficulty of obtaining stocks and ultimately the sale of finished products.

Again there are trade-offs. If there is plenty of labour, equipment and raw materials available, the stocks of finished goods need not be as high because they can be quickly produced. If those basic resources are not as readily available then stocks of finished goods must be kept at a higher level. Stock management techniques are fully explained in the next chapter.

## Managing Plant and Equipment

Most plant and equipment is used over a long period of time and much of it is very costly. Therefore, purchasing decisions about these resources must be made carefully. As technology changes at an ever-increasing rate, there is a chance that plant may become obsolescent very quickly. Where the construction of the plant takes a long time, there is a particular problem. Motor-car assembly lines, for instance, may take two or three years to build and may have to be planned five years ahead. The techniques specially used in planning capital expenditure of this kind are explained in chapter 10.

## Owning the Right Quantity of Assets

How does a firm decide on the optimum quantities of its assets to hold? There is obviously a relationship between the level of sales made and the level of assets required. Having either too many assets or too few assets will both create problems and solve problems.

**Too many assets** will mean that there is no need to be aggressive in credit collection. There's plenty of cash available so it doesn't matter. You'll never run out of stock and there are no slowdowns in production due to a shortage of raw materials. The high inventory levels will mean excellent customer service. A customer who wants a pair of size fourteen shoes in purple with pink spots has a choice of styles. But all of those assets are costing money to finance. The potential profitability of the situation is being squandered. If capital costs 18 per cent per annum and inventories are $500 000 more than they need to be, there is a wastage of $90 000 a year in the cost of financing the inventory.

**Too few assets** will also cause problems. This will mean that it is desperate to collect from its debtors. Collection can become a little too aggressive and customers become offended. There are stock-outs and customers become annoyed at the narrow range available. There are production scheduling problems because of the shortage of plant, equipment and labour.

### The Operating Cycle

Quite clearly, the aim is to operate somewhere between these two extremes. To understand the key concepts involved in working capital management, we must consider what is usually called the **operating cycle** or **cash-to-cash cycle**. This refers to the process involved in going from holding cash to purchasing or manufacturing goods, selling it and collecting the proceeds. Figure 8.1 shows the phases in this cycle:

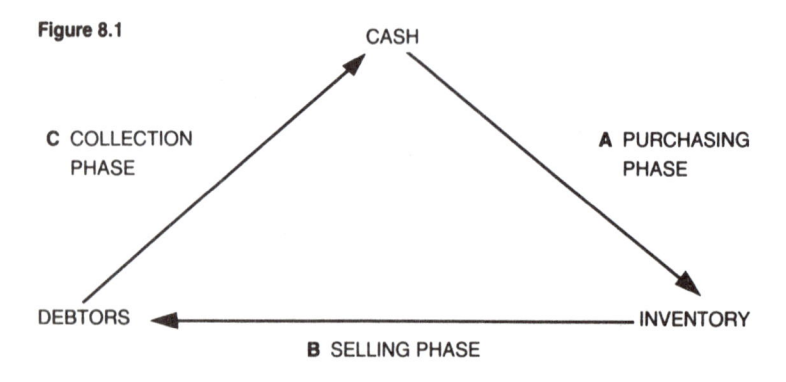

Figure 8.1

```
                    CASH
                   /    \
                  /      \
    C COLLECTION /        \ A PURCHASING
    PHASE      /          \ PHASE
              /            \
             /              ↘
    DEBTORS ←——————————————— INVENTORY
                B SELLING PHASE
```

## The Three Phases of the Operating Cycle

The operating cycle starts with cash being used to purchase or manufacture goods. The length of this purchasing part of the cycle will be measured as the time between the business paying for the goods and the time when they are available for sale.

This purchasing phase may take only a short period of time if the goods are purchased ready for sale. In a greengrocer's shop, for example, the purchasing phase may be only half a day. If the business buys on terms, this may be a negative figure. For example, a business may buy on 30-day terms, and have delivery in 7 days. This means that the purchasing phase is -23 days. The goods are available for sale 23 days before the payment takes place. Clearly, this type of situation is very beneficial to financing that business.

On the other hand, some manufacturers, who buy raw materials, may take several months to have the goods in saleable condition.

The second phase of the cycle is the selling phase. The length of this phase depends largely upon the nature of the goods and the usual turnover rates in that industry.

Once the goods are sold, the cycle enters its third phase, collecting the proceeds from the customer. The length of this phase will be determined by the trading terms and the reliability of the customer. Once the money is collected, the business has an expanded amount of cash due to the profit, and the cycle starts again.

In the simplest cycle situations where a retailer pays for the goods as they are supplied, then is able to sell them straight away, the whole cycle may take zero days. This is the case with greengrocers and fishmongers who buy for cash at the wholesale markets in the morning and have the goods in the shop the same day.

A manufacturer, however, may have to pay for raw materials which then take several weeks or months to be converted into finished goods. By the time they are sold, and the proceeds are collected, several months may pass.

## The Stock Turn or Stock Turnover Rate

The length of the selling phase is the average length of time between the availability of stock for sale and its actual sale, converting the inventory into debtors. Again, this depends largely upon the nature of the stock concerned. Some products naturally sell faster than others. In the furniture business, stock commonly takes three months to sell. This means that the selling phase is ninety days. In the antiques business some items may take a year to sell, a selling phase of 365 days. Fortunately, the fishmonger does better than that; his selling phase is likely to be only a day or two. A measure of the length of this phase is the stockturn or stock turnover rate.

$$\text{Stock turnover rate} = \frac{\text{Cost of goods sold}}{\text{Average stock}}$$

The cost of goods sold is the aggregate cost of all stock sold during the year. The average stock figure may be calculated on an ongoing basis or just as a simple opening stock/closing stock average for the year. The stock turnover rate is, then, the number of times the stock turns over for the year. If, for instance, a hardware shop sells goods for the year which cost $1 600 000 and the average stock is $400 000, the stock turnover rate is:

$$\text{Stock turnover rate} = \frac{\$1\,600\,000}{400\,000}$$
$$= 4 \text{ times}$$

Since there are about 360 days in a year we can convert this into an average number of selling days by dividing it into 360 days.

That is:

$$\text{Average selling days} = \frac{360 \text{ days}}{4 \text{ times}}$$
$$= 90 \text{ days}$$

For this hardware shop an item takes on average ninety days to sell. This is fairly typical of the hardware business. If the hardware shop had purchasing days of negative twenty, at this stage its operating cycle is minus twenty plus ninety, equaling seventy days long and it still has to collect from the customers.

Consider the impact of this on financing costs, assuming that the weighted average cost of capital is 20 per cent per annum in this case. We have said that the average stock held by the hardware shop is $400 000. At 20 per cent per annum the financing cost of this stock is $80 000 a year. If, in another business with the same cost of goods sold for the year, there was a faster stock-turn, say eight times a year, the financing cost would be lower. If

$$\text{Stock turnover rate} = \frac{\text{Cost of goods sold}}{\text{Average stock}}$$

then it is true that

$$\text{Average stock} = \frac{\text{Cost of goods sold}}{\text{Stock turnover rate}}$$

So in the second business:

$$\text{Average stock} = \frac{\$1\,600\,000}{8}$$
$$= \$200\,000$$

The financing of that smaller average stock will cost only $40 000 giving that firm a competitive advantage. So increasing the stock turnover rate will reduce costs.

However, if margins have to be cut to do that, the financing costs saved must be matched against the lost revenue.

## Debtors Turnover Rate

Once the sales are made on credit we enter the final phase of the process, collecting the proceeds from the debtors. Most credit terms these days are nominally thirty days. However, many firms take liberties with this arrangement and it tends to stretch out towards an average of forty-five days or more. Apart from offering discount incentives for rapid payment, there is not much that can be done about this without offending the customers. Just as stock turnover rates can be measured in the firm, so can debtors' turnover rates.

$$\text{Debtors' turnover rate} = \frac{\text{Credit sales}}{\text{Average debtors}}$$

Credit sales represents the total amount of debtors that you have had over the year, because every credit sale creates a debtor and that is the only way they are created. The average debtors may be an ongoing monthly average or a simple start of year/end of year average. So if the firm has made credit sales of $2 400 000 for the year and the average debtors figure is $400 000, the debtors' turnover figure will be

$$\text{Debtors' turnover rate} = \frac{\$2\,400\,000}{\$400\,000}$$
$$= 6 \text{ times}$$

This can be converted into days as we did with the stock turnover rate:

$$\frac{360 \text{ days}}{6 \text{ times}} = 60 \text{ days}$$

If the customers are supposed to be on thirty-days terms this is not too good. Perhaps credit control or collection procedures are not as they should be. Given the 20 per cent cost of capital that average debtors figure of $400 000 is costing

$$20\% \text{ of } \$400\,000 = \$80\,000 \text{ a year to finance}$$

If the average length of payments outstanding could be cut back to forty-five days, this would mean that the turnover rate would be increased to

$$\frac{360 \text{ days}}{45 \text{ days}} = 8 \text{ times a year}$$

$$\text{If the debtors turnover rate} = \frac{\text{Credit sales}}{\text{Average debtors}}$$

then it must be true that

$$\text{Average debtors} = \frac{\text{Credit sales}}{\text{Debtors' turnover rate}}$$

And the average debtors in our example will drop to

$$\text{Average debtors} = \frac{\$2\,400\,000}{8 \text{ times}}$$
$$= \$300\,000$$

The cost of financing this average debtors level at 20 per cent per annum is only

$$20\% \text{ of } \$300\,000 = \$60\,000 \text{ a year}$$

as opposed to the earlier sum of $80 000. Thus, by simply speeding up the process of debt collection, there is a saving of $20 000 in financing cost. Also, by collecting the debts faster, you lessen the chances of losing money in bad debts.

Of course, the best possible situation for the seller is to be able to sell entirely for cash, which would remove the problem of financing debtors or trying to collect the proceeds. Service stations and supermarkets usually operate on a cash basis and removal of the burden of financing debtors allows them to sell on lower margins than would otherwise be possible.

Quite clearly it is of great advantage to a business to be able to keep its operating cycle as short as possible. A business which pays cash for its supplies and waits three weeks for delivery, then has a stock turnover rate of four times a year and a debtors turnover rate of six times a year has an operating cycle of 171 days. That is, it has a

| | |
|---|---|
| purchasing phase of | 21 days |
| selling phase of | 90 days |
| collection phase of | 60 days |
| TOTAL | 171 days |

A competitor who buys on thirty-days terms and stretches it out to forty-five days, insists on delivery within seven days, has a stock turnover rate of six times a year and a debtors turnover of nine times a year has an operating cycle of only sixty-two days. That is, it has a

| | |
|---|---|
| purchasing phase of | −38 days |
| selling phase of | 60 days |
| collection phase of | 40 days |
| TOTAL | 62 days |

The second firm obviously has much lower costs in financing its current assets because of its shorter operating cycle. It is much more efficient in its management of working capital..

Of course, the best type of business to be in is one where its buying power is great enough to insist on very favourable terms from suppliers, it has a fast stock-turn and sells only for cash. One large Australian retailer insists that suppliers give it sixty-days credit from the date of supply. It turns its stock over ten times a year and sells only for cash. Therefore its operating cycle is

| | |
|---|---|
| purchasing phase | −60 days |
| selling phase | +36 days |
| collection phase | zero |
| TOTAL | −24 days |

That is, the money is always collected (with profit) an average of 24 days before the goods sold have to be paid for. No wonder the business is more than moderately profitable.

Just about any business can be made more profitable by speeding up its operating cycle. However, there are pitfalls and trade-offs to be wary of.

Businesses rarely improve their overall profitability by cutting margins. Slashing margins really chops into your contribution margin with a disproportionate effect on profits. For instance, imagine that a firm has been selling $800 000 worth of stock with a gross margin of $200 000. A cut of 10 per cent in price will cut the gross margin to $120 000 which reduces it and the contribution margin by 80 000 divided by 200 000, or 40 per cent.

A 20 per cent price-cut would reduce the margin by 80 per cent, and a 25 per cent price-cut gets rid of all of the margin.

If, in order to speed up their payments, additional pressure is placed on debtors, they may be lost as customers to the opposition. Some customers are very skillful at playing off suppliers against one another and buying where they can get away with stretching the conditions a little. Others are not fully in control of their activities and have to be watched, or even nurtured to make sure that they don't go out of business entirely.

Due to the international reputation of some of our crashed high-fliers the Americans are inclined to think that Australians are all like that. Recently, when I was in America I was asked 'How do you put an Aussie into a small business? 'I don't know', I said, puzzled.

'Buy him a big business and wait', was the answer.

Here are some general rules for working capital management.

1   Keep stocks as low as possible without running the risk of stock-outs.

2. Keep debtors as low as possible without offending them by over-aggressive collection.
3. Don't keep larger cash balances than you need but have sufficient available for emergencies.
4. Try to keep the operating cycle as short as possible.

# 9

## Inventory Control

As we saw in the previous chapter, it is essential to keep current assets under tight control and this applies particularly to inventories. But isn't it possible that having large stocks of some commodity that suddenly escalates in price may make you a fortune?

You've probably heard of Freddy. Freddy bought $500,000 worth of a rare metal called inconium. Everybody said he was mad, because his company would take fifty years to use it all. However, the opportunity was there and Freddy liked to take a punt occasionally. Well, just after he bought it, NASA technicians found that the metal could be used to line booster rockets so that it made them re-usable, with huge cost savings. The search was on world-wide for the comparatively few stocks of inconium that were available and Freddy found the world beating a path to his door. The opening offer was for $10 million, but Freddy refused, saying that he needed the inconium in the combustion chambers of his incinerators. The Americans did not fool around and the offer rose to $12 million, then $14 million, then $20 million; but still Freddy held out. At $25 million Freddy could resist no longer. He sold the inconium, closed up the business and retired, filthy rich, to the sands of the Sunshine Coast.

Sounds like a fairy story, doesn't it? It is!

If I had a kilo of inconium for every time I've heard a variation of this story I'd be able to sell it to NASA and retire. Things just don't happen like that. In one case in a thousand, there may be some small upward valuation in the stocks held of some item or another, gold perhaps. In the other 999 cases, stocks held will tend to decrease in value because they become damaged, outdated or stale. That's the way it is with stock - the more you've got, the more it costs you to look after it, and the more likely it is that you'll make losses. Therefore inventories must be carefully planned.

## The Golden Rule of Inventory Planning

There is a golden rule that should always be followed in inventory planning. **Never keep more inventory than is required to satisfy customers.** A small inventory:

- Requires little storage space, therefore it will keep down storage costs like insurance and warehousing;
- Has a much lower risk of obsolescence, pilfering and deterioration;
- Requires a smaller investments of capital, keeping financing costs down and reducing the target profit needed.

A large inventory does have some benefits, however. It reduces the risk of stock-outs. In a retail situation, a customer who finds that the shop does not have the required item is not only lost on that sale, but probably will not return next time they want a similar item. With a manufacturer, stock-outs of a component of raw material can bring the whole factory to a halt, leading to stand-downs of workers and idle resources. A motor-car assembly line, for instance, can be brought to a halt simply by the lack of a small component like seat belts or wheel nuts. Larger inventories usually mean fewer re-orders, with a saving in paperwork and administrative costs. Buying in larger quantities and carrying higher stocks can lead to quantity discounts which may more than offset the additional costs of carrying larger inventory levels.

## Factors to Consider in Planning Inventories

The planning of inventory must take all of these factors into consideration to find an optimum level for inventories of all kinds, which will maximise profitability. Here are some steps to follow.

1. Determine which inventory items are worth the cost and time spent in planning. Small low-priced, low-quantity items may not be worth spending time and resources in planning.

2. Find the safety stock or minimum stock levels acceptable for each particular item of stock which is worthy of planning.

3. Calculate economic order quantities for these planned items. The method for doing this is shown in this chapter.

4. Develop simpler rules for those items where careful planning is not justified.

Many businesses are faced with inventories of thousands of different items. The average motor car, for instance, has about ten thousand different parts. Some are common to all models, others peculiar to only one. Careful inventory planning is an expensive procedure and it may not be worth the trouble and cost for all items because the real savings are less than the cost of the processes involved. So full analysis and planning may be restricted to those items

- where there is a danger of obsolescence;
- where the inventory is expensive; or
- where there are special storage requirements.

Some inventory items are subject to special problems of obsolescence or deterioration. Quite obviously, over-stocking of these items is asking for trouble. Fashion goods are a major trap. What can you do if you've stocked up with thousands of mini skirts and the fashion changes? Now full-length skirts are in. You can't just sew bits on the bottom. You're caught; they're not worth a cracker. Products which deteriorate quickly create a similar problem. If a fishmonger is at the fish market one morning and sees a mountain of flounder selling at only $1 a kilo, it would probably not be sensible for him to buy all of it. In his case, buying the 'right' quantities is critical.

Many items create special storage problems, either because of their nature or size. If you're going into the second-hand jumbo jet business you'll need quite a large warehouse. Frozen foods and other products requiring refrigeration are another problem. It is no good buying quantities beyond your storage capacity. Providing additional refrigerated storage is extremely expensive. Other products can be just as difficult. One manufacturer of chocolate biscuits had major problems in storing liquid chocolate for the biscuits. It had to be kept at exactly the right temperature so that it did not burn and become bitter or harden in the tank. After trying all sorts of techniques, the company decided not to store it at all and to get deliveries as required on a 'just-in-time' basis.

## The ABC Method of Inventory Control

Items which are expensive to buy justify careful planning because they cost so much to finance. One of the most common methods used in deciding which items to plan is the ABC method. In most organisations a small range of inventory items, because of their cost and frequency of use, represents a large proportion of the total inventory value. The ABC method requires that:

1 Those items that represent a high proportion of inventory investment are identified. They are tagged A items. They might be only 10 per cent of the total items but represent 75 per cent of the total inventory value.

2 A second group of items representing less valuable parts of the inventory are then identified. These are the B items. In a typical situation this may be another 5 per

cent of the items, with a value of 15 per cent of the total inventory.

3   The rest are the C items. The other 85 per cent of inventory items may be in this category, with only 10 per cent of the total value. These items are probably not worth spending money and time in planning in detail.

So detailed planning would be restricted to those items regarded as being in the A or B categories. Detailed planning will require the calculation of lead time, sales rate, safety stocks, average inventory levels and order quantities.

## Lead Time and Safety Stocks

**Lead time** is the time taken to receive goods after an order has been placed. It is possible to predict lead time fairly accurately if the supplier and the mode of transportation are reliable. However, particularly where the stock is coming from overseas, lead times can be difficult to establish with any reliability. Once I was expecting a container of glass from France. The suppliers were wonderfully reliable and it arrived on the wharf a week earlier than predicted. And there it sat. The container parked on top of mine had been declared 'black' by the unions. They couldn't move mine without first moving that one, and it took six weeks to liberate it. So lead times must always be regarded with some suspicion.

As we saw in chapter 7, the expected annual sales are established in the sales budget. This can be quite easily converted into a daily sales rate by dividing by the number of working days in the year. So if the firm works on 300 days of the year and expects to sell 18 000 of the items for the year, the daily sales figure should be 18 000 divided by 300, which equals sixty per day. This assumes, of course, that sales will be evenly spread throughout the year. If there is reason to believe that sales will not be evenly spread, calculations can be made on a seasonal rather than an annual basis.

If the lead time was certain and the sales rate was even, reordering would be easy. If, for example, we always did sell sixty items per day and we had a fully reliable lead time of ten days, we could always re-order when stocks were down to 600 items knowing that as the stock reached zero, the new shipment would arrive. But that's not going to happen and we will probably have to allow for safety stocks to cover this situation.

The average inventory level must be the mid-point between the highest level and lowest level of inventory. The high point occurs when a new order arrives and the low point immediately before the new order arrives. So if the inventory is never allowed to fall below 100 units and each order is for 500 units at a time, the inventory fluctuates between 100 and 600 units. The average inventory is therefore 350 units.

As we saw earlier, if lead time is certain because of complete reliability, and daily sales are perfectly consistent, we could let the stocks run down to nothing with complete confidence that more stock will arrive to prevent a stock-out. Lead times fluctuate because of transport problems, suppliers' stock problems, industrial disputes and every possible manifestation of Murphy's Law. A solution to this situation is to establish safety stock levels. Later in this chapter we shall consider 'just-in-time' inventory organisation. That method eliminates all safety stocks, but it requires special conditions to operate.

**Safety stocks** establish a cushion of spare stock to cover the chance that shipments may be delayed. The simplest method of calculating the safety stock is for management to arbitrarily decide that it will be a certain number of days' sales or usage. A slightly more sophisticated way is to base it on the fluctuations between maximum daily usage and average daily usage. For instance, assume that Huggan Industries determines that for the item in question:

Maximum daily usage is 80 units
Average daily usage is 60 units
Lead time is 20 days

The safety stock is computed at:

(Maximum daily usage − average daily usage) x lead time

That is:

(80 units − 60 units) x 20
= 20 units x 20
= 400 units

Clearly, this is a satisfactory basis only if the major problem is uncertainty in the daily usage. If the problem is uncertainty in the lead time itself, a totally different approach is required. Using the data above and assuming that although lead time is normally twenty days, there is a possibility it could be as long as thirty-five days, we could calculate safety stock as:

(Maximum lead time − usual lead time) x average daily usage

That is:

(35 days − 20 days) x 60 units
= 15 days x 60 units
= 900 units

To be absolutely safe, we may want to multiply by the maximum daily usage rather than the average daily usage. This would give us 1 200 units as a safety stock. If we are as conservative as that, there is little point in planning at all as savings are likely to be marginal. When you consider the large sums tied up in inventory, however, savings can be enormous. The Firestone Tyre and Rubber Co. in the United States was able to cut its inventory by $300 million, saving $60 million a year in financing costs.

Once the safety stock is calculated, the re-order point is easy to find:

> Re-order point = Safety stock + (lead time x average daily usage or sales)

So if Huggan Industries decides that a safety stock of 400 units is adequate, the re-order point will be:

> Re-order point = 400 + (20 days x 60 units)
> = 1 600 units

The business would re-order when stock on hand plus those in transit equals 1 600 units.

## Economic Order Quantity

Quite obviously there are costs attached to re-ordering and costs attached to carrying stocks. There must be some optimum size of order which minimises the total cost. This optimum size order is called the **economic order quantity**.

Ordering costs are the administrative expenses of making an order and receiving it, including inspection and quality control. These costs would normally be calculated on a 'per order' basis.

Carrying costs are the costs of holding stocks. They include, for example, financing costs for the inventory; warehousing costs including wages, handling and insurance; and allowances for loss, damage and obsolescence. Carrying costs are normally calculated on a 'per unit per annum' basis.

It is fairly obvious that if you have infrequent large orders you will keep down the ordering costs but the comparatively high average inventories will lead to higher carrying costs. On the other hand, frequent small orders will keep average inventories down, decreasing carrying costs, but will increase ordering costs. The fact is that in this type of situation the lowest total costs occur at the point where the total ordering costs are equal to the total carrying costs. Graphically, this relationship is shown in Figure 9.1.

**Figure 9.1 Cost Behaviour of Inventories**

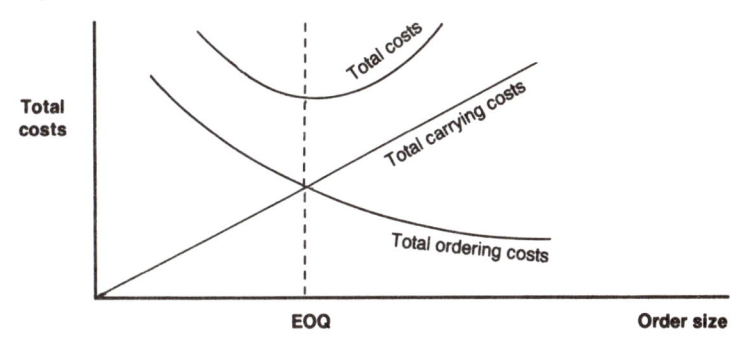

[Graph showing Total costs on y-axis and Order size on x-axis, with curves for Total costs, Total carrying costs, and Total ordering costs intersecting at EOQ]

As order size increases, orders are less frequent and total ordering costs decrease. As order size increases, average inventory will be higher, so carrying costs increase. Total costs are lowest at the point where total ordering costs and total carrying costs are the same. This is at the economic order quantity (EOQ).

This proposition can be proven by means of a tabular example. Assume that for its Petunia Patch doll, Gruesome Industries has the following data:

| | |
|---|---|
| Annual sales | 20 000 dolls |
| Order cost | $100 per order |
| Carrying cost | 25 cents per doll per annum |

We will assume that no safety stocks are necessary. The following can be seen from Figure 9.2:

1. Total ordering cost rises with the number of orders.
2. Total carrying cost falls with the number of orders. This occurs because more frequent orders means less stock in each order, so smaller inventories.
3. At five orders per year, each order of 4 000 dolls, the total carrying costs and total ordering costs are equal.

**Figure 9.2**
**Economic order quantity**

| No. of orders per year | Dolls per order | Average inventory | Total ordering costs | Total carrying costs | Total cost |
|---|---|---|---|---|---|
|  |  |  | $ | $ | $ |
| 1 | 20 000 | 10 000 | 100 | 2 500 | 2 600 |
| 2 | 10 000 | 5 000 | 200 | 1 250 | 1 450 |
| 3 | 6 667 | 3 333 | 300 | 833 | 1 133 |
| 4 | 5 000 | 2 500 | 400 | 625 | 1 025 |
| 5 | 4 000 | 2 000 | 500 | 500 | 1 000 |
| 6 | 3 333 | 1 667 | 600 | 417 | 1 017 |
| 7 | 2 857 | 1 429 | 700 | 357 | 1 057 |
| 10 | 2 000 | 1 000 | 1 000 | 250 | 1 250 |

4   At that same level the total costs are minimised at $1,000. Therefore this is the economic order quantity.

5   At the economic order quantity, total ordering costs are equal to total carrying costs.

Because of this relationship, it is possible, using differential calculus, to reduce the EOQ calculation to a formula. This formula is

$$EOQ = \sqrt{\frac{2 \times D \times Co}{Cc}}$$

where D = annual demand
Co = cost per order
Cc = carrying cost per unit per annum

Applying this formula to the example used in the table earlier we have

$$EOQ = \sqrt{\frac{2 \times 20\,000 \times 100}{0.25}}$$
$$= \sqrt{16\,000\,000}$$
$$= 4000 \text{ units}$$

Now that's a lot easier than using tables or graphs, isn't it?

As long as you know the annual demand, the cost per order and the carrying cost per unit, you can always work out the economic order quantity. Not surprisingly, computer programs are readily available for this purpose. Where there are variable discounts for quantity, however, this simple formula cannot be used except to obtain an estimate. More sophisticated computer programs are available which allow for discounts, safety stocks and variable lead times.

### Economic Production Run

Where the item is produced in a factory rather than purchased, the same formula can be used, except that the set-up cost is substituted for the ordering cost. This will produce the **economic production run** - the size of production run which minimises costs:

$$\text{Economic production run} = \sqrt{\frac{2 \times D \times Sc}{Cc}}$$

where D = annual demand
Sc = set-up cost
Cc = carrying cost per unit per annum

Therefore, if the Dinkeye Co. Ltd which produces Garry Gumnut books has the following data:

| | |
|---|---|
| Annual demand | 15 000 units |
| Set-up costs | $150 |
| Carrying costs | $2 per unit per annum |

the economic size production run will be

$$\text{Economic production run} = \sqrt{\frac{2 \times 15\,000 \times 150}{2}}$$
$$= \sqrt{2\,250\,000}$$
$$= 1500 \text{ units}$$

In order to minimise total costs, the company should make production runs of 1 500 units at a time.

## Just-in-Time Inventory Management

The development of the just-in-time approach to inventory planning is a good example of going back to basics. While the Americans developed the EOQ model, the Japanese questioned whether a manufacturer should be carrying inventory at all at the component end of the process.

The aim of 'just-in-time' is to reduce the quantity of raw materials or components as close as possible to zero. This has a number of implications. One is that your suppliers must be kept closely informed about your needs. Ideally they will have copies of your production schedules, and will know exactly when you will require a particular component. Ultimately the manufacturer and the supplier are hooked up by computer so that the supplier is continuously aware of the situation. The firms that supply the supplier may also need to be involved in this process.

The industrial relations climate is also critical to the just-in-time method. If you decide that you will not bring in stocks of a particular component until the day before you intend to use them, that's fine. But remember that what you are doing is getting rid of your safety stocks. If you needed safety stocks before, why don't you need them now? Don't just take the risk; it is advisable to run a full training program for your staff and the people who work for the suppliers. In the light of the industrial relations record of many Australian industries, it may be a very brave decision to rely on just-in-time methods until there is a change of attitude by both workers and management.

There is no doubt, however, that eventually we must introduce efficient methods like just-in-time. If we don't we will never be able to effectively compete in world markets. The Japanese motor firm Toyota is usually quoted as the best example of using the technique. Before the introduction of just-in-time, the company kept about a month's supply of components on hand. This was costly, not only because of financing, but also because of storage and deterioration. These days the average time that a component spends in inventory before use is less than a week, and some components arrive only twenty minutes before use. (Yes, I know that sometimes yours arrive ten minutes before they're required, but in Toyota's case it's intentional.)

If you can't fully implement the technique, any move in that direction is worthwhile. In 1979 British Leyland, one of the world's more troubled companies, had massive storage problems at its largest truck plant. There were rented stores everywhere at massive cost, and stock control was a nightmare. A firm of management consultants recommended the building of new storage facilities with automated handling equipment. The cost was over $50 million. Before spending such a large sum, the company decided to try cutting inventory instead. Over a two-year period, inventory was cut by half and all of the rented storage space was closed down. British Leyland was able to save not only the $50 million worth of capital investment, but also annual costs of millions of dollars.

In your firm you may not be able to improve matters on that scale, but remember that even small savings add up. If you can find a way that stock can be cut by even $10 000 you will enable the company to use that $10 000 in a more useful way, and the cost savings on the use of that $10 000 will be about $2 000 a year, not just for one year, but permanently. The more you save the company amounts of that order, the more valuable you are to the company. Never be afraid to put forward ideas and let people know they ar your ideas.

Remind them of what you have done. W.S. Gilbert once wrote:

*If you wish in this world to advance,*

*Your merits you're bound to enhance,*

*You must stir it and stump it,*

*And blow your own trumpet,*

*Or trust me, you haven't a chance.*

Where an item is too small or cheap to warrant the use of sophisticated calculation methods, informal methods may be used. One common method is the 'two-bin method". You have a bin out on the factory floor and one in the store. When the factory bin is empty, you wheel in the full one from the store. You take the empty bin out to the store and get it filled up. In many small engineering works, this is the only method of stock management used and it is generally very effective. Sometimes automatic re-ordering on particular dates is used, especially where usage is consistent. Some major items like fuel stocks are often handled in this way.

Now that we have looked in some detail at the management of current assets we will consider fixed assets.

# 10

# Planning Capital Expenditure

We have seen in chapters 8 and 9 that it is necessary to be very careful in planning current assets. Considering that the costs involved in obtaining and holding fixed assets are somewhat larger, you might expect that the planning is even more complex and careful. You'd be right! Of course, no matter how good the accounting techniques are, you still have to use your common sense or you can be bitten.

I mean, I know it was too good to be true. But you get led on by your own greed. I asked all the right questions. Got all the right answers, too. I suppose.

'How high are the earnings?'

'Captive market. Make 'em as high as you like.'

'Are the earnings guaranteed?'

'Just about. There's not much alternative.'

'What about reliability? How long will it last?'

'Long as you and me, mate.'

'What about maintenance costs?'

'Not much. Spot of paint here. Spot of paint there. I tell you it's a dead-set winner. You can't lose.'

But I did lose, didn't I? Still we can write it off to experience. It's not every day that you buy the Sydney Harbour Bridge.

## Capital Budgeting

Capital budgeting is the process of planning capital expenditure. It will be used whenever the purchase of fixed assets of significant cost is proposed. Will we buy a new truck? Will we build a new assembly line? Will we replace that old plant? Will we move the factory to that new site? Capital budgeting looks at the answers to these sorts of questions.

If funds are to be spent on some asset which is going to cost a great deal of money and be with the company for some years, it is important that the decision be made on a logical basis. The basis of the decision must be a comparison of the anticipated benefits arising from the asset, with the outlays required. The future benefits will be expressed in dollar terms as future cash inflows.

As always, predicting what will happen in the future is fraught with danger, and even the best information prepared in good faith can be wrong. Where someone has a vested interest in making the proposal appear more beneficial than it is, real problems can arise. Sometimes people 'championing' a project can close their eyes to its dangers and shortcomings. Estimates must be made of the initial cash outlay or investment, the net cash flows which will arise from the investment, and the economic life of the asset.

The initial cash outlay or investment consists of all costs incurred in getting the asset operational. This includes the initial purchase price of the asset or assets, any costs of transporting it to its place of use, installation costs and setting-up costs, including trial runs. Since this total initial outlay figure is a critical one in the calculations which are made before the project is begun, any distortion of this figure through cost overruns or poor estimation can turn a good project into a bad one.

Once the project or asset is operating it will produce cash inflows. When the cash outflows are matched against inflows, net cash flow figures are obtained. Estimating what these figures will be, perhaps several years ahead, is a difficult and dangerous task. Most managers not emotionally involved in a project will err on the conservative side, perhaps understating likely inflows and overstating likely outflows. It is usual to use cash flow information rather than estimated profits because cash flows are what is required to make repayments on any financing. Profit calculations include 'book entries' like depreciation which have nothing to do with the decision since the whole initial cost of the project is part of the decision-making calculation.

The economic life of the asset is the period of time in which the firm can expect to receive benefits from the asset. It may be a shorter period than the physical life of the asset because the asset may become obsolescent due to changes in technology or market conditions. Generally speaking it is not wise to expect economic returns beyond ten years.

Over time, the popular methods used in assessing capital projects have changed. However, in all methods what is important is the relationship between the initial outlay and the net cash flows. The methods that we will consider here are the unadjusted payback period; the accounting rate of return; discounted cash flow methods (DCF); and time-adjusted payback.

**The Payback Method**

The unadjusted payback period is a classic method still used by many planners. Some people regard it as old-fashioned and unscientific, but some of this country's greatest businessmen still use it. The aim of the method is to calculate how long it takes for the project to make sufficient cash inflows to pay back the initial outlay. Most companies that use this method set down 'rules of thumb' for its use. One large business group tells its managers that if payback looks possible in one year, they must go ahead with the project. If payback is possible within three years, it must be submitted to top management. If payback looks unlikely within three years, forget it. To take an example, consider the case of Colossal Industries Ltd which is considering the installation of a new plant. It has been investigating the project for weeks. The initial cost, including installation, will be $480 000. Estimated net cash inflows from the project are as follows:

>    Year 1   $200 000
>    Year 2   $240 000
>    Year 3   $200 000
>    Year 4   $200 000
>    Year 5   $120 000

It is intended to scrap the plant after five years.

The payback period is the length of time it takes to recoup the outlay of $480 000. At the end of two years $440 000 will have been recouped, so payback occurs some time in the third year. If we assume that the cash flows are evenly spread through the year, the $40 000 still required will be obtained one-fifth of the way through the third year. So the payback period is 2.2 years. If two mutually exclusive projects were being considered, the project chosen would be the one with the shorter payback period.

The payback method gives an advantage to projects that have early returns, it is easy to understand and simple to calculate. Its big weakness is that it ignores what happens after payback is achieved. Some projects may be slow in returns in the early years but give massive returns in later years. These will seldom be approved under a payback rule. **After all the profitability of a project occurs after payback. At payback there is zero profit.**

Another problem is that the selection of the payback period is arbitrary. It is often claimed that it ignores the time pattern of the cash flows, but this is not strictly true as it gives great advantage to projects with early returns.

## The Accounting Rate of Return

A second method of assessing capital projects is the accounting rate of return. Consider two mutually exclusive projects under consideration by Super Industries Ltd. Project A has an initial outlay of $300 000 and an economic life of five years. At the end of that time it will have a scrap value of $50 000. The after tax profits for the next five years are expected to be $20 000, $200 000, $175 000, $175 000, and $40 000. Project B has an initial outlay of $350 000 and the economic life is five years with no scrap value at the end. The after-tax profits are expected to be $100 000 in each year. The company has a cost of capital of 18 per cent and requires a return on assets of at least 20 per cent per annum.

The accounting rate of return is usually calculated as the simple percentage rate of return shown by profits on the initial outlay for the project. That is:

$$\frac{\text{Average after-tax profit}}{\text{Initial outlay}} \%$$

The project will be approved only if it meets the rate of return required by management. Here are the calculations for projects A and B.

*Project A* Average after-tax profit is

$$\frac{\$\ 20\,000 + 200\,000 + 175\,000 + 175\,000 + 40\,000}{5}$$
$$= \$122\,000$$

Since the initial outlay is $300 000 this represents an accounting rate of return of

$$\frac{\$\ 122\,000}{300\,000} = 40.7\%$$

which easily exceeds the required rate of return of 20 per cent.

*Project B* Average profit is $100,000 on an outlay of $350,000. So the accounting rate of return is

$$\frac{\$\,100\,000}{350\,000} = 28.6\%$$

which is also well above the required rate of return.

Since only one project can be chosen we would accept the one with the higher rate of return, Project A. We may even be tempted to look at their payback periods; 2.46 years for Project A and 3.50 years for Project B.

The accounting rate of return method is easily calculated and understood. It does have some weaknesses, however.

1. The cut-off rate of return required is set arbitrarily.

2. The size or scale of the investment is ignored, except that it is probably the scale which makes projects mutually exclusive.

3. The method does not consider the timing of the cash flows. The basis used is average profits and it does not matter whether these are concentrated in the early years or the late years of the project. Since profits could be re-invested if they are earned in the early years, there are additional benefits in receiving early profits.

4. Profit is used rather than cash flow as the basis of return. This profit calculation depends on accounting conventions and principles which may not be relevant to the decision. For one thing it is net of 'book entry' items like depreciation on the project, which will cause true returns to be understated.

## Discounted Cash Flow Methods (DCF)

A third way of assessing capital projects is by using discounted cash flow methods (DCF). These depend upon a concept referred to as the **time preference for money**.

If I offer you two choices:

- You can have $1000 now or
- You can have the same $1000 in a year's time

you will most probably choose to take the money now. If you don't, you are not like the rest of us. This indicates that there is a time preference for money. Why does it exist? Probably because the money received immediately could be invested without risk at say, 10 per cent, and become $1 100 in a year's time.

What if I have $1 000 now that can be invested at 10 per cent compound interest for three years? How much would I have to be offered in three years' time to wait for the money, rather

than take the $1000 now? At compound interest of 10 per cent the $1000 will grow to be $1100 at the end of the first year; $1210 at the end of the second year; and $1331 at the end of the third year. So if I was offered either $1000 now, or $1331 at the end of three years with no risk, I would have no preference. Both offers are equally attractive. If the right to the $1331 in three years' time was up for sale, the maximum amount that I would pay for it now is $1000. If I paid more than $1000 for it, I would be worse off than investing my $1000 at the 10 per cent rate available. If I paid, for example, $1050 for the right to $1331 in three years' time, I would get less than the equivalent of a 10 per cent rate of return on my money.

The $1000 value that this investment now has is called its **present value**. I can always calculate the present value of any investment by applying a formula which is the reciprocal of the compound interest formula. This process is called **discounting**. Fortunately for us non-mathematicians, a table is available which shows factors for the various rates of return and time periods (see Table 10.1).

**Table 10.1**
**Present Value Tables**

*Present value of $1*

| Years Hence | 1% | 2% | 4% | 6% | 8% | 10% | 12% | 14% | 15% | 16% | 18% |
|---|---|---|---|---|---|---|---|---|---|---|---|
| 1 | 0.990 | 0.980 | 0.962 | 0.943 | 0.926 | 0.909 | 0.893 | 0.877 | 0.870 | 0.862 | 0.847 |
| 2 | 0.980 | 0.961 | 0.925 | 0.890 | 0.857 | 0.826 | 0.797 | 0.769 | 0.756 | 0.743 | 0.718 |
| 3 | 0.971 | 0.942 | 0.889 | 0.840 | 0.794 | 0.751 | 0.712 | 0.675 | 0.658 | 0.641 | 0.609 |
| 4 | 0.961 | 0.924 | 0.855 | 0.792 | 0.735 | 0.683 | 0.636 | 0.592 | 0.572 | 0.552 | 0.516 |
| 5 | 0.951 | 0.906 | 0.822 | 0.747 | 0.681 | 0.621 | 0.567 | 0.519 | 0.497 | 0.476 | 0.437 |
| 6 | 0.942 | 0.888 | 0.790 | 0.705 | 0.630 | 0.564 | 0.507 | 0.456 | 0.432 | 0.410 | 0.370 |
| 7 | 0.933 | 0.871 | 0.760 | 0.665 | 0.583 | 0.513 | 0.452 | 0.400 | 0.376 | 0.354 | 0.314 |
| 8 | 0.923 | 0.853 | 0.731 | 0.627 | 0.540 | 0.467 | 0.404 | 0.351 | 0.327 | 0.305 | 0.266 |
| 9 | 0.914 | 0.837 | 0.703 | 0.592 | 0.500 | 0.424 | 0.361 | 0.308 | 0.284 | 0.263 | 0.225 |
| 10 | 0.905 | 0.820 | 0.676 | 0.558 | 0.463 | 0.386 | 0.322 | 0.270 | 0.247 | 0.227 | 0.191 |
| 11 | 0.896 | 0.804 | 0.650 | 0.527 | 0.429 | 0.350 | 0.287 | 0.237 | 0.215 | 0.195 | 0.162 |
| 12 | 0.887 | 0.788 | 0.625 | 0.497 | 0.397 | 0.319 | 0.257 | 0.208 | 0.187 | 0.168 | 0.137 |
| 13 | 0.879 | 0.773 | 0.601 | 0.469 | 0.368 | 0.290 | 0.229 | 0.182 | 0.163 | 0.145 | 0.116 |
| 14 | 0.870 | 0.758 | 0.577 | 0.442 | 0.340 | 0.263 | 0.205 | 0.160 | 0.141 | 0.125 | 0.099 |
| 15 | 0.861 | 0.743 | 0.555 | 0.417 | 0.315 | 0.239 | 0.183 | 0.140 | 0.123 | 0.108 | 0.084 |
| 16 | 0.853 | 0.728 | 0.534 | 0.394 | 0.292 | 0.218 | 0.163 | 0.123 | 0.107 | 0.093 | 0.071 |
| 17 | 0.844 | 0.714 | 0.513 | 0.371 | 0.270 | 0.198 | 0.146 | 0.108 | 0.093 | 0.080 | 0.060 |
| 18 | 0.836 | 0.700 | 0.494 | 0.350 | 0.250 | 0.180 | 0.130 | 0.095 | 0.081 | 0.069 | 0.051 |
| 19 | 0.828 | 0.686 | 0.475 | 0.331 | 0.232 | 0.164 | 0.116 | 0.083 | 0.070 | 0.060 | 0.043 |
| 20 | 0.820 | 0.673 | 0.456 | 0.312 | 0.215 | 0.149 | 0.104 | 0.073 | 0.061 | 0.051 | 0.037 |
| 21 | 0.811 | 0.660 | 0.439 | 0.294 | 0.199 | 0.135 | 0.093 | 0.064 | 0.053 | 0.044 | 0.031 |
| 22 | 0.803 | 0.647 | 0.422 | 0.278 | 0.184 | 0.123 | 0.083 | 0.056 | 0.046 | 0.038 | 0.026 |
| 23 | 0.795 | 0.634 | 0.406 | 0.262 | 0.170 | 0.112 | 0.074 | 0.049 | 0.040 | 0.033 | 0.022 |
| 24 | 0.788 | 0.622 | 0.390 | 0.247 | 0.158 | 0.102 | 0.066 | 0.043 | 0.035 | 0.028 | 0.019 |
| 25 | 0.780 | 0.610 | 0.375 | 0.233 | 0.146 | 0.092 | 0.059 | 0.038 | 0.030 | 0.024 | 0.016 |
| 26 | 0.722 | 0.598 | 0.361 | 0.220 | 0.135 | 0.084 | 0.053 | 0.033 | 0.026 | 0.021 | 0.014 |
| 27 | 0.764 | 0.586 | 0.347 | 0.207 | 0.125 | 0.076 | 0.047 | 0.029 | 0.023 | 0.018 | 0.011 |
| 28 | 0.757 | 0.574 | 0.333 | 0.196 | 0.116 | 0.069 | 0.042 | 0.026 | 0.020 | 0.016 | 0.010 |
| 29 | 0.749 | 0.563 | 0.321 | 0.185 | 0.107 | 0.063 | 0.037 | 0.022 | 0.017 | 0.014 | 0.008 |
| 30 | 0.742 | 0.552 | 0.308 | 0.174 | 0.099 | 0.057 | 0.033 | 0.020 | 0.015 | 0.012 | 0.007 |
| 40 | 0.672 | 0.453 | 0.208 | 0.097 | 0.046 | 0.022 | 0.011 | 0.005 | 0.004 | 0.003 | 0.001 |
| 50 | 0.608 | 0.372 | 0.141 | 0.054 | 0.021 | 0.009 | 0.003 | 0.001 | 0.001 | 0.001 | |

**Table 10.1 (continued)**

*Present value of $1*

| Years Hence | 20% | 22% | 24% | 25% | 26% | 28% | 30% | 35% | 40% | 45% | 50% |
|---|---|---|---|---|---|---|---|---|---|---|---|
| 1 | 0.833 | 0.820 | 0.806 | 0.800 | 0.794 | 0.781 | 0.769 | 0.741 | 0.714 | 0.690 | 0.667 |
| 2 | 0.694 | 0.672 | 0.650 | 0.640 | 0.630 | 0.610 | 0.592 | 0.549 | 0.510 | 0.476 | 0.444 |
| 3 | 0.579 | 0.551 | 0.524 | 0.512 | 0.500 | 0.477 | 0.455 | 0.406 | 0.364 | 0.328 | 0.296 |
| 4 | 0.482 | 0.451 | 0.423 | 0.410 | 0.397 | 0.373 | 0.350 | 0.301 | 0.260 | 0.226 | 0.198 |
| 5 | 0.402 | 0.370 | 0.341 | 0.328 | 0.315 | 0.291 | 0.269 | 0.223 | 0.186 | 0.156 | 0.132 |
| 6 | 0.335 | 0.303 | 0.275 | 0.262 | 0.250 | 0.227 | 0.207 | 0.165 | 0.133 | 0.108 | 0.088 |
| 7 | 0.279 | 0.249 | 0.222 | 0.210 | 0.198 | 0.178 | 0.159 | 0.122 | 0.095 | 0.074 | 0.059 |
| 8 | 0.233 | 0.204 | 0.179 | 0.168 | 0.157 | 0.139 | 0.123 | 0.091 | 0.068 | 0.051 | 0.039 |
| 9 | 0.194 | 0.167 | 0.144 | 0.134 | 0.125 | 0.108 | 0.094 | 0.067 | 0.048 | 0.035 | 0.026 |
| 10 | 0.162 | 0.137 | 0.116 | 0.107 | 0.099 | 0.085 | 0.073 | 0.050 | 0.035 | 0.024 | 0.017 |
| 11 | 0.135 | 0.112 | 0.094 | 0.086 | 0.079 | 0.066 | 0.056 | 0.037 | 0.025 | 0.017 | 0.012 |
| 12 | 0.112 | 0.092 | 0.076 | 0.069 | 0.062 | 0.052 | 0.043 | 0.027 | 0.018 | 0.012 | 0.008 |
| 13 | 0.093 | 0.075 | 0.061 | 0.055 | 0.050 | 0.040 | 0.033 | 0.020 | 0.013 | 0.008 | 0.005 |
| 14 | 0.078 | 0.062 | 0.049 | 0.044 | 0.039 | 0.032 | 0.025 | 0.015 | 0.009 | 0.006 | 0.003 |
| 15 | 0.065 | 0.051 | 0.040 | 0.035 | 0.031 | 0.025 | 0.020 | 0.011 | 0.006 | 0.004 | 0.002 |
| 16 | 0.054 | 0.042 | 0.032 | 0.028 | 0.025 | 0.019 | 0.015 | 0.008 | 0.005 | 0.003 | 0.002 |
| 17 | 0.045 | 0.034 | 0.026 | 0.023 | 0.020 | 0.015 | 0.012 | 0.006 | 0.003 | 0.002 | 0.001 |
| 18 | 0.038 | 0.028 | 0.021 | 0.018 | 0.016 | 0.012 | 0.009 | 0.005 | 0.002 | 0.001 | 0.001 |
| 19 | 0.031 | 0.023 | 0.017 | 0.014 | 0.012 | 0.009 | 0.007 | 0.003 | 0.002 | 0.001 | |
| 20 | 0.026 | 0.019 | 0.014 | 0.012 | 0.010 | 0.007 | 0.005 | 0.002 | 0.001 | 0.001 | |
| 21 | 0.022 | 0.015 | 0.011 | 0.009 | 0.008 | 0.006 | 0.004 | 0.002 | 0.001 | | |
| 22 | 0.018 | 0.013 | 0.009 | 0.007 | 0.006 | 0.004 | 0.003 | 0.001 | 0.001 | | |
| 23 | 0.015 | 0.010 | 0.007 | 0.006 | 0.005 | 0.003 | 0.002 | 0.001 | | | |
| 24 | 0.013 | 0.008 | 0.006 | 0.005 | 0.004 | 0.003 | 0.002 | 0.001 | | | |
| 25 | 0.010 | 0.007 | 0.005 | 0.004 | 0.003 | 0.002 | 0.001 | 0.001 | | | |
| 26 | 0.009 | 0.006 | 0.004 | 0.003 | 0.002 | 0.002 | 0.001 | | | | |
| 27 | 0.007 | 0.005 | 0.003 | 0.002 | 0.002 | 0.001 | 0.001 | | | | |
| 28 | 0.006 | 0.004 | 0.002 | 0.002 | 0.002 | 0.001 | 0.001 | | | | |
| 29 | 0.005 | 0.003 | 0.002 | 0.002 | 0.001 | 0.001 | 0.001 | | | | |
| 30 | 0.004 | 0.003 | 0.002 | 0.001 | 0.001 | 0.001 | | | | | |
| 40 | 0.001 | | | | | | | | | | |
| 50 | | | | | | | | | | | |

## Table 10.2
**Present Value of an Annuity**

*Present value of $1 received annually for N years*

| Years (N) | 1% | 2% | 4% | 6% | 8% | 10% | 12% | 14% | 15% | 16% | 18% |
|---|---|---|---|---|---|---|---|---|---|---|---|
| 1 | 0.990 | 0.980 | 0.962 | 0.943 | 0.926 | 0.909 | 0.893 | 0.877 | 0.870 | 0.862 | 0.847 |
| 2 | 1.970 | 1.942 | 1.886 | 1.833 | 1.783 | 1.736 | 1.690 | 1.647 | 1.626 | 1.605 | 1.566 |
| 3 | 2.941 | 2.884 | 2.775 | 2.673 | 2.577 | 2.487 | 2.402 | 2.322 | 2.283 | 2.246 | 2.174 |
| 4 | 3.902 | 3.808 | 3.630 | 3.465 | 3.312 | 3.170 | 3.037 | 2.914 | 2.855 | 2.798 | 2.690 |
| 5 | 4.853 | 4.713 | 4.452 | 4.212 | 3.993 | 3.791 | 3.605 | 3.433 | 3.352 | 3.274 | 3.127 |
| 6 | 5.795 | 5.601 | 5.242 | 4.917 | 4.623 | 4.355 | 4.111 | 3.889 | 3.784 | 3.685 | 3.498 |
| 7 | 6.728 | 6.472 | 6.002 | 5.582 | 5.206 | 4.868 | 4.564 | 4.288 | 4.160 | 4.039 | 3.812 |
| 8 | 7.652 | 7.325 | 6.733 | 6.210 | 5.747 | 5.335 | 4.968 | 4.639 | 4.487 | 4.344 | 4.078 |
| 9 | 8.566 | 8.162 | 7.435 | 6.802 | 6.247 | 5.759 | 5.328 | 4.946 | 4.772 | 4.607 | 4.303 |
| 10 | 9.471 | 8.983 | 8.111 | 7.360 | 6.710 | 6.145 | 5.650 | 5.216 | 5.019 | 4.833 | 4.494 |
| 11 | 10.368 | 9.787 | 8.760 | 7.887 | 7.139 | 6.495 | 5.937 | 5.453 | 5.234 | 5.029 | 4.656 |
| 12 | 11.255 | 10.575 | 9.385 | 8.384 | 7.536 | 6.814 | 6.194 | 5.660 | 5.421 | 5.197 | 4.793 |
| 13 | 12.134 | 11.343 | 9.986 | 8.853 | 7.904 | 7.103 | 6.424 | 5.842 | 5.583 | 5.342 | 4.910 |
| 14 | 13.004 | 12.106 | 10.563 | 9.295 | 8.244 | 7.367 | 6.628 | 6.002 | 5.724 | 5.468 | 5.008 |
| 15 | 13.865 | 12.849 | 11.118 | 9.712 | 8.559 | 7.606 | 6.811 | 6.142 | 5.847 | 5.575 | 5.092 |
| 16 | 14.718 | 13.578 | 11.652 | 10.106 | 8.851 | 7.824 | 6.974 | 6.265 | 5.954 | 5.669 | 5.162 |
| 17 | 15.562 | 14.292 | 12.166 | 10.477 | 9.122 | 8.022 | 7.120 | 6.373 | 6.047 | 5.749 | 5.222 |
| 18 | 16.398 | 14.992 | 12.659 | 10.828 | 9.372 | 8.201 | 7.250 | 6.467 | 6.128 | 5.818 | 5.273 |
| 19 | 17.226 | 15.678 | 13.134 | 11.158 | 9.604 | 8.365 | 7.366 | 6.550 | 6.198 | 5.877 | 5.316 |
| 20 | 18.046 | 16.351 | 13.590 | 11.470 | 9.818 | 8.514 | 7.469 | 6.623 | 6.259 | 5.929 | 5.353 |
| 21 | 18.857 | 17.011 | 14.029 | 11.764 | 10.017 | 8.649 | 7.562 | 6.687 | 6.312 | 5.973 | 5.384 |
| 22 | 19.660 | 17.658 | 14.451 | 12.042 | 10.201 | 8.772 | 7.645 | 6.743 | 6.359 | 6.011 | 5.410 |
| 23 | 20.456 | 18.292 | 14.857 | 12.303 | 10.371 | 8.883 | 7.718 | 6.792 | 6.399 | 6.044 | 5.432 |
| 24 | 21.243 | 18.914 | 15.247 | 12.550 | 10.529 | 8.985 | 7.784 | 6.835 | 6.434 | 6.073 | 5.451 |
| 25 | 22.023 | 19.523 | 15.622 | 12.783 | 10.675 | 9.077 | 7.843 | 6.873 | 6.464 | 6.097 | 5.467 |
| 26 | 22.795 | 20.121 | 15.983 | 13.003 | 10.810 | 9.161 | 7.896 | 6.906 | 6.491 | 6.118 | 5.480 |
| 27 | 23.560 | 20.707 | 16.330 | 13.211 | 10.935 | 9.237 | 7.943 | 6.935 | 6.514 | 6.136 | 5.492 |
| 28 | 24.316 | 21.281 | 16.663 | 13.406 | 11.051 | 9.307 | 7.984 | 6.961 | 6.534 | 6.152 | 5.502 |
| 29 | 25.066 | 21.844 | 16.984 | 13.591 | 11.158 | 9.370 | 8.022 | 6.983 | 6.551 | 6.166 | 5.510 |
| 30 | 25.808 | 22.396 | 17.292 | 13.765 | 11.258 | 9.427 | 8.055 | 7.003 | 6.566 | 6.177 | 5.517 |
| 40 | 32.835 | 27.355 | 19.793 | 15.046 | 11.925 | 9.799 | 8.244 | 7.105 | 6.642 | 6.234 | 5.548 |
| 50 | 39.196 | 31.424 | 21.482 | 15.762 | 12.234 | 9.915 | 8.304 | 7.133 | 6.661 | 6.246 | 5.554 |

**Table 10.2 (continued)**

*Present value of $1 received annually for N years*

| Years (N) | 20% | 22% | 24% | 25% | 26% | 28% | 30% | 35% | 40% | 45% | 50% |
|---|---|---|---|---|---|---|---|---|---|---|---|
| 1 | 0.833 | 0.820 | 0.806 | 0.800 | 0.794 | 0.781 | 0.769 | 0.741 | 0.714 | 0.690 | 0.667 |
| 2 | 1.528 | 1.492 | 1.457 | 1.440 | 1.424 | 1.392 | 1.361 | 1.289 | 1.224 | 1.165 | 1.111 |
| 3 | 2.106 | 2.042 | 1.981 | 1.952 | 1.923 | 1.868 | 1.816 | 1.696 | 1.589 | 1.493 | 1.407 |
| 4 | 2.589 | 2.494 | 2.404 | 2.362 | 2.320 | 2.241 | 2.166 | 1.997 | 1.849 | 1.720 | 1.605 |
| 5 | 2.991 | 2.864 | 2.745 | 2.689 | 2.635 | 2.532 | 2.436 | 2.220 | 2.035 | 1.876 | 1.737 |
| 6 | 3.326 | 3.167 | 3.020 | 2.951 | 2.885 | 2.759 | 2.643 | 2.385 | 2.168 | 1.983 | 1.824 |
| 7 | 3.605 | 3.416 | 3.242 | 3.161 | 3.083 | 2.937 | 2.802 | 2.508 | 2.263 | 2.057 | 1.883 |
| 8 | 3.837 | 3.619 | 3.421 | 3.329 | 3.241 | 3.076 | 2.925 | 2.598 | 2.331 | 2.108 | 1.922 |
| 9 | 4.031 | 3.786 | 3.566 | 3.463 | 3.366 | 3.184 | 3.019 | 2.665 | 2.379 | 2.144 | 1.948 |
| 10 | 4.192 | 3.923 | 3.682 | 3.571 | 3.465 | 3.269 | 3.092 | 2.715 | 2.414 | 2.168 | 1.965 |
| 11 | 4.327 | 4.035 | 3.776 | 3.656 | 3.544 | 3.335 | 3.147 | 2.752 | 2.438 | 2.185 | 1.977 |
| 12 | 4.439 | 4.127 | 3.851 | 3.725 | 3.606 | 3.387 | 3.190 | 2.779 | 2.456 | 2.196 | 1.985 |
| 13 | 4.533 | 4.203 | 3.912 | 3.780 | 3.656 | 3.427 | 3.223 | 2.799 | 2.468 | 2.204 | 1.990 |
| 14 | 4.611 | 4.265 | 3.962 | 3.824 | 3.695 | 3.459 | 3.249 | 2.814 | 2.477 | 2.210 | 1.993 |
| 15 | 4.675 | 4.315 | 4.001 | 3.859 | 3.726 | 3.483 | 3.268 | 2.825 | 2.484 | 2.214 | 1.995 |
| 16 | 4.730 | 4.357 | 4.033 | 3.887 | 3.751 | 3.503 | 3.283 | 2.834 | 2.489 | 2.216 | 1.997 |
| 17 | 4.775 | 4.391 | 4.059 | 3.910 | 3.771 | 3.518 | 3.295 | 2.840 | 2.492 | 2.218 | 1.998 |
| 18 | 4.812 | 4.419 | 4.080 | 3.928 | 3.786 | 3.529 | 3.304 | 2.844 | 2.494 | 2.219 | 1.999 |
| 19 | 4.844 | 4.442 | 4.097 | 3.942 | 3.799 | 3.539 | 3.311 | 2.848 | 2.496 | 2.220 | 1.999 |
| 20 | 4.870 | 4.460 | 4.110 | 3.954 | 3.808 | 3.546 | 3.316 | 2.850 | 2.497 | 2.221 | 1.999 |
| 21 | 4.891 | 4.476 | 4.121 | 3.963 | 3.816 | 3.551 | 3.320 | 2.852 | 2.498 | 2.221 | 2.000 |
| 22 | 4.909 | 4.488 | 4.130 | 3.970 | 3.822 | 3.556 | 3.323 | 2.853 | 2.498 | 2.222 | 2.000 |
| 23 | 4.925 | 4.499 | 4.137 | 3.976 | 3.827 | 3.559 | 3.325 | 2.854 | 2.499 | 2.222 | 2.000 |
| 24 | 4.937 | 4.507 | 4.143 | 3.981 | 3.831 | 3.562 | 3.327 | 2.855 | 2.499 | 2.222 | 2.000 |
| 25 | 4.948 | 4.514 | 4.147 | 3.985 | 3.834 | 3.564 | 3.329 | 2.856 | 2.499 | 2.222 | 2.000 |
| 26 | 4.956 | 4.520 | 4.151 | 3.988 | 3.837 | 3.566 | 3.330 | 2.856 | 2.500 | 2.222 | 2.000 |
| 27 | 4.964 | 4.524 | 4.154 | 3.990 | 3.839 | 3.567 | 3.331 | 2.856 | 2.500 | 2.222 | 2.000 |
| 28 | 4.970 | 4.528 | 4.157 | 3.992 | 3.840 | 3.568 | 3.331 | 2.857 | 2.500 | 2.222 | 2.000 |
| 29 | 4.975 | 4.531 | 4.159 | 3.994 | 3.841 | 3.569 | 3.332 | 2.857 | 2.500 | 2.222 | 2.000 |
| 30 | 4.979 | 4.534 | 4.160 | 3.995 | 3.842 | 3.569 | 3.332 | 2.857 | 2.500 | 2.222 | 2.000 |
| 40 | 4.997 | 4.544 | 4.166 | 3.999 | 3.846 | 3.571 | 3.333 | 2.857 | 2.500 | 2.222 | 2.000 |
| 50 | 4.999 | 4.545 | 4.167 | 4.000 | 3.846 | 3.571 | 3.333 | 2.857 | 2.500 | 2.222 | 2.000 |

Across the top of the present value table are percentage figures indicating the rate of return, and down the left-hand side of the table are indicators of the number of time periods (usually years) into the future in which the cash flow will occur. By applying the factor given in the table, to the amount to be received, we can calculate the present value of the amount. For example, earlier we said that the present value of an amount of $1331 to be received in three years' time where the available investment rate was 10 per cent was $1000. We can verify this by using the table. However, rounding off the factors to three decimal places may mean that they are not exactly correct. In our example, we will look across the top of the table to the 10 per cent column. Looking down to the factor for year three we find that it is 0.751. When this factor is multiplied by the cash flow to be received we get:

0.751 x $1331 = $999.58

We know that this should be $1000 but the difference is not significant. The difference is due to the factor being rounded off to three decimal places.

Consider an investment which costs $2000 right now and which pays a single cash flow benefit of $2800 in four years' time. We know that we can get 14 per cent rate of return on similar investments. Is it a good investment?

Simply use the discounting approach on the cash flows by applying factors from the table. The factor for 14 per cent after four years is 0.592.

| (a) Year | (b) Net cash flow | (c) Factor | (d) Present value of cash flow (b x c) |
|---|---|---|---|
| 4 | $2800 | 0.592 | $1657.60 |

| | | |
|---|---|---|
| So the present value of the investment is | | $1657.60 |
| Less: the initial cost | | $2000.00 |
| Net present value | | $(342.40) |

The net present value is the present value of the cash flows less the initial cost of the investment. In this case the net present value is negative. That does not mean that the investor would make a loss, after all the investment does give $2800 return for an outlay of $2000, a profit of $800. However, the negative net present value means that the investment does not give a rate of return of the required 14 per cent compound interest.

Where a constant amount is to be received over a number of years, this is referred to as annuity. The present value of an annuity can be calculated by using factors from Table 10.2. Consider, for example, the present value of an annuity of $1000 to be received each year for five years when we know that similar investments pay a 16 per cent rate of return per annum. The approach is similar:

| (a) Year | (b) Net cash flow | (c) Factor | (d) Present value of cash flow (b x c) |
|---|---|---|---|
| 1-5 | $1000 | 3.274 | $3274 |

The present value of the annuity is $3274 and that is the maximum amount that I could pay for it and receive a 16 per cent compound rate of return. If the investment can be purchased for $3000 it has a positive net present value of $274. This means that it will pay a 16 per cent rate of return per annum and provide an extra $274.

The reason that we used the annuity table here rather than Table 10.1 is that in this case the $1000 was to be received in every year. In the earlier examples there was only a single cash flow in one future year.

If the discounting approach can be used in assessing this type of investment, it can also be used in assessing capital investment by firms in exactly the same way. We will apply it to Project A and Project B considered earlier under the accounting rate of return method. There are three main approaches that we will consider. All use the discounting method as a basis. They are the net present value method, the internal rate of return method and cost/benefit ratios.

## The Net Present Value Method

In the net present value method we set up the cash flows just as we did with the simple investments, and apply the factors from the present value tables in exactly the same way (see Figures 10.1 and 10.2). We will use factors from the 20 per cent column as that is the required rate of return. For Project B we can use the annuity table as the next cash flow is the same in each year.

**Figure 10.1**
**Project A**

| Year | Cash flow* | Factor | PV of cash flow |
|---|---|---|---|
| 1 | $70 000 | 0.833 | $58 310 |
| 2 | 250 000 | 0.694 | 173 500 |
| 3 | 225 000 | 0.579 | 130 275 |
| 4 | 225 000 | 0.482 | 108 450 |
| 5 | 140 000† | 0.402 | 56 280 |
| | | Present value | 526 815 |
| | | Less: Initial outlay | 300 000 |
| | | Net present value | $226 815 |

*The cash flows are profit + depreciation added back, as it is not a cash outflow.
†Includes scrap value of $50 000.

**Figure 10.2**
**Project B**

| Year | Cash flow* | Factor | PV of cash flow |
|---|---|---|---|
| 1-5 | $150 000 | 2.991 | $448 650 |
| | | Less: Initial outlay | 350 000 |
| | | Net present value | $ 98 650 |

*Profit + depreciation added back, as it is not a cash outflow.

In both cases the depreciation ($50 000 per annum) has been added back to the profit as this involves no outflow of cash. We are using cash flow information, not profit, in this method. As we can see, both Project A and Project B have positive net present values, so both have a rate of return substantially higher than 20 per cent; how much higher we shall see when we use the internal rate of return method. If forced to choose between the projects, we would go for the project with the higher positive net present value. In this case it is Project A by a substantial margin, with a net present value of $226 815.

## The Internal Rate of Return Method

The present value approach showed us that the rate of return offered by Project A and Project B was substantially above 20 per cent. The internal rate of return method actually calculates the rate of return that the project yields on a compound basis.

We have seen that when a project does not yield the desired rate of return, it shows a negative net present value. When it gives more than the required level, it shows a positive net present value. It should be no surprise to you, then, to learn that when it gives exactly the desired rate of return the net present value is zero. So the internal rate of return is the discounting rate which produces a zero net present value. Because it is simpler, we will take Project B first.

Project B has the same return in every year so we can use the annuity table to find the internal rate of return. First we find the factor by dividing the initial outlay by the annual net cash flows (remembering to add back depreciation to the profit if that has not already been done):

$$\text{Annuity factor} = \frac{\text{Initial outlay}}{\text{Annual net cash flow}}$$

$$= \frac{350\,000}{150\,000}$$

$$= 2.33$$

Now since the earnings occur over a five-year period, we check across the five-year line in the table until we come to the 2.33 factor. When we do this we find that 2.33 is not there, the closest each side are 2.436 (30 per cent) and 2.220 (35 per cent). So we know that the rate of return is somewhere between 30 and 35 per cent. This may be sufficient.

If we want to be more accurate we can interpolate between the figures. The factor we calculated is almost exactly half-way between the two factors we found.

Therefore so is the rate. The internal rate of return is about 37.5 per cent.

Project A is more difficult and involves the use of trial and error calculations to find the rate which gives a zero net present value. Since this project had a higher net present value than Project B, it is obvious that its internal rate of return is also higher. Our first step is to calculate the net present value at a 45 per cent rate of return (see Figure 10.3)

Using a 45 per cent discounting rate, the project yields a positive net present value, so the internal rate of return must be above 45 per cent per annum. This may be sufficient to convince us that Project A is an excellent project which is clearly superior to Project B. However, for reasons of tidiness we may want to try the project at a 50 per cent rate of return. The procedure is the same as before. However, since the discounting rates ar outside the scope of our tables, we must obtain discount factors from a more comprehensive table.

At 50 per cent discounting rate (see Figure 10.4), the project yields a negative net present value of ($12 680). So it does not give an internal rate of return of 50 per cent per annum. At 45 per cent per annum there is a net present value of $13 790. Since these are almost equally either side of zero, we could assume that the true internal rate of return is about half-way between 45 per cent and 50 per cent, about 48 per cent.

**Figure 10.3**

| Year | Cash flow | Factor | PV of cash flow |
|---|---|---|---|
| 1 | $70 000 | 0.690 | $48 300 |
| 2 | 250 000 | 0.476 | 119 000 |
| 3 | 225 000 | 0.328 | 73 800 |
| 4 | 225 000 | 0.226 | 50 850 |
| 5 | 140 000 | 0.156 | 21 840 |
|   |   | Present value | $313 790 |
|   |   | Less: Initial outlay | 300 000 |
|   |   | Net present value | $13 790 |

**Figure 10.4**

| Year | Cash flow | Factor | PV of cash flow |
|---|---|---|---|
| 1 | $70 000 | 0.667 | $46 690 |
| 2 | 250 000 | 0.444 | 111 000 |
| 3 | 225 000 | 0.296 | 66 600 |
| 4 | 225 000 | 0.198 | 44 550 |
| 5 | 140 000 | 0.132 | 18 480 |
|   |   | Present value | $287 320 |
|   |   | Less: Initial outlay | 300 000 |
|   |   | Net present value | $(12 680) |

Internal rate of return decisions are usually made in conjunction with a 'hurdle rate of return.' A rate of return is set which is acceptable. If the project passes that hurdle rate it is accepted; if it fails to pass the hurdle rate it is rejected. If the hurdle rate for the two projects here was 20 per cent, then both projects are acceptable. However, since they are mutually exclusive projects, Project A would be accepted because its internal rate of return is considerably higher.

### Cost/Benefit Ratio

Another way of expressing the present value results is to put them in the form of a cost/benefit ratio or profitability index. Once the net present value is calculated, the calculation of the index is simple. The formula is

$$\text{Cost/benefit ratio} = 1 + \frac{\text{Net present value}}{\text{Initial investment outlay}}$$

If the net present value of the project is positive, the formula must produce a cost/benefit ratio above one. If the NPV is negative, the cost/benefit ratio must be below one. So the basis of decision-making is that the project is viable if the cost/benefit ratio is one or greater. If there are two or more projects under consideration, the best is the project with the highest cost/benefit ratio.

Earlier, we saw that at the 20 per cent discounting rate, Project A, which costs $300 000, had a NPV of $226 815; and Project B, which costs $350 000, had a NPV of $98 650. Using the cost/benefit formula for the two projects:

Project A

$$\text{Cost/benefit ratio} = 1 + \frac{\$226\,815}{\$300\,000} = 1.76$$

Project B

$$\text{Cost/benefit ratio} = 1 + \frac{\$98\,650}{\$350\,000} = 1.28$$

Although both projects have cost/benefit ratios above one, Project A is clearly superior.

Quite clearly net present value, internal rate of return and cost/benefit ratios all give us the same information expressed in slightly different ways. In practice, therefore, there would be no point in making the calculation in all three ways as they will give the same advice.

## Time-Adjusted Payback

The last method of assessing capital projects that we will consider is time-adjusted payback. Early in this chapter we looked at the use of the relatively unsophisticated technique of unadjusted payback. With the advent of DCF techniques, some decision-makers have adopted a special type of payback calculation which converts the cash flows into their present value equivalents, then calculates the payback period on them.

It is claimed that this overcomes payback's failure to consider the cost of capital and the pattern of returns. If we reconsider the payback example on a time-adjusted basis, the first thing to do is select a rate of return, which will usually be the cost of capital and convert the expected cash flows into present value equivalents. We will assume that the cost of capital is 18 per cent (see Figure 10.5).

**Figure 10.5**
**COLOSSAL INDUSTRIES LTD**

| Year | Cash flow | Factor | PV of cash flow | Cumulative PV |
|---|---|---|---|---|
| 1 | $200 000 | 0.847 | $169 400 | $169 400 |
| 2 | 240 000 | 0.718 | 172 320 | 341 720 |
| 3 | 200 000 | 0.609 | 121 800 | 463 520 |
| 4 | 200 000 | 0.516 | 103 200 | 566 720 |
| 5 | 120 000 | 0.437 | 52 440 | 619 160 |

Now all we have to do is use the cumulative present value column to find the payback period. The initial outlay required is $480 000. Using the present value figures, we can see that by the end of the first three years the present value of cash flow recouped is $463 520. So time-adjusted payback will occur at about 3.2 years. Although this method overcomes some of the objections to unadjusted payback, it has not gained general acceptance.

## Capital Rationing

In theory, a business should proceed with all projects that have a positive net present value because these projects have a return which is greater than the cost of funds. In practice however, there may be constraints which make it necessary to select from possible projects. This may occur, for example, because management is conservative and is not prepared to risk further borrowings. In that instance, capital could only be raised through share issues and there is a danger that this could affect control of the company.

Another constraint may be that it is company policy only to expand into new projects using retained earnings, and these are limited. Another may be that lenders want to impose restrictions or gain security which is unacceptable to management.

In these situations, capital for projects is limited and this capital rationing means that only some projects can be selected. The method of ranking projects in these circumstances depends upon management. Linear programming models are sometimes used to find the most profitable combinations of projects, given the limitations. Clearly, projects that fail to meet one of the company's requirements, such as a prescribed hurdle rate, or which have a cost/benefit ratio of less than one, will be rejected. Beyond that, most managers would prefer to rank projects on the basis of net present value.

Perhaps this is the time to add a word of warning. Many of the techniques that we have looked at in this chapter carry the mystique of mathematical models. Give us a few formulas and calculations and the whole thing takes on the air of precision and exactitude of a science laboratory. This is a trap. It is nothing of the sort. Remember all of these calculations, regardless of method used, depend upon two basic inputs:

- educated guesses about what the future cash flows and profits will be from the asset or project; and
- the arbitrary selection of some required rate of return.

As we said at the outset in this chapter, the need for accuracy and quality in the information used, particularly estimated future cash flows, cannot be overstated. It doesn't matter how sophisticated the model used and whether it uses whole banks of new-generation computers producing wads of projections. If the input was garbage, the output is garbage. If it is, you may find that you don't have to buy the Harbour Bridge to lose your money.

# 11

# Controlling Expenses

In chapter 7 we looked at the budgeting process in some detail and we briefly considered some aspects of expense control through responsibility accounting. We now look at this important area in more detail.

If you are an executive, you will have certain responsibilities. These could be anything from making sure the Cafe-Bar machine is switched on, to administering a budget of fifty million dollars. Every executive has different responsibilities.

Once in my early days as a brash young executive, I was given an opportunity to show my efficiency. We had occupied a new building but the drainage wasn't working too well. A contract had been let for a firm to put in new drains but the starting date was unclear. The phone rang.

'Eric Smith, Managing Director's personal assistant.'

'Are you the bloke that's supposed to deal with the drains contract?'

'That's correct.'

'Well just thought you oughta know we're making a start on you today. I'll have a trench digger out there about twelve. Right?'

'Yes, that'll be fine.'

Thoughts of this massive machine mixing it with the Mercs and BMWs in the car park made me shiver. I dashed from office to office announcing the impending arrival of the monster and ordering that all cars be moved into the street. They would have to chance it with the parking officers for one day. Even the Managing Director was not exempt. The Roller was parked out on the curb.

I sat anxiously awaiting the rumble of machinery, the roaring of powerful diesel engines. None came. Then at about twelve-thirty there was a timid knock on my door.

'Excuse me, Mr Smith, I was asked to tell you I'm here.'

'Who are you?'

'Name's Perkins. I'm the trench digger.'

It was a man with a spade.

## Responsibility Centres

The responsibilities in managing an organisation can be divided in numerous ways. However, most organisations have sub-units or responsibility centres, which are described as either cost centres, revenue centres, profit centres or investment centres.

## Cost Centres

In a cost centre the manager has the authority to control costs but is not authorised to change revenue or the investment in resources. The manager's performance is measured in terms of whether the objectives of the centre are achieved within the budgeted expenses. The manager really has to be considered in terms of his total performance (how effectively the required output or performance is achieved); and his financial performance (which refers to keeping actual expense levels within those set by the budget).

Generally these objectives will be consistent, but sometimes where total performance is based on service objectives, they may be in conflict. A chief librarian, for instance, may operate the library very 'successfully' in financial terms because it operates well within its budget. But if this is achieved by keeping the library closed for half the week, then total performance could be criticised.

## Revenue Centres

In a revenue centre the manager is mainly responsible for marketing. Financial performance is measured in terms of whether the centre achieves its budgeted levels of revenue. The manager is expected to make the decisions necessary for reaching the budgeted revenue figures but is not responsible for production expenses. However, the manager may still be responsible for budgeted expenses which are part of the revenue-producing operations, such as sales staff salaries and promotion.

## Profit Centres

In a profit centre the manager has responsibility for the centre producing a certain budgeted profit figure. Since this profit results from both revenue and costs, the manager has responsibility and control over both and should make decisions that produce the best profit result. There are other responsibilities for which this manager may be responsible such as staff morale, research and development, and maintenance of plant, but financial performance will be measured in terms of the bottom line. Did the manager achieve the budgeted levels of profit?

## Investment Centres

The investment centre is the ultimate in managerial responsibility. The manager is responsible not only for costs, revenues, profitability, morale and all of those other things, there is the additional responsibility to see that assets are adequately used. This implies that the manager has authority to purchase new assets and dispose of old ones. The manager's performance will be judged mainly according to whether the investment centre produces a satisfactory rate of return on the assets used and meets the budgeted residual income levels.

In general (although there are exceptions), a plant manager or department manager is in charge of a cost centre; a sales manager is in charge of a revenue centre, a general manager is in charge of a profit centre; a managing director is in charge of an investment centre.

## Performance Reports

Under the principles of responsibility accounting, managers will receive reports which cover their responsibilities. The manager of a cost centre will receive a cost report which shows the budgeted costs and variances from those costs so that the variances can be investigated. A revenue centre manager will receive sales and revenue reports with sales and revenue variances highlighted. Again, any unfavorable variances can be investigated. The profit centre manager will receive reports showing revenue and costs and variances in both as they affect profit. It is a case of each manager receiving information relevant to his or her responsibility.

In chapter 7 we saw the format that a performance report might take. The critical part of a report such as this is the variances from budget. Figure 11.1 shows a performance report with variances. After reading this report, what should the manager do that is, after having a stiff drink? The way to proceed is as follows:

1   Determine whether the variance is significant.

2   If it is significant, try to discover what caused it.

3   Take action to overcome the problem. This could be anything from having the budget figures changed, to correcting an error in the figures, or dismissing employees.

**Figure 11.1**
**PAPER MACHINE 1**
Performance Report July 19-- (30 working days)

| Production (tonnes) | Budget | Actual | Variance | Variance |
|---|---|---|---|---|
|  | 2 100 | 1 980 | (120) | 5.7 |
| Expenses | $ | $ | $ | % |
| Direct labour - normal | 18 600 | 19 500 | (900) | (4.8) |
|        - overtime | — | 1 600 | (1 600) | (+) |
| Maintenance | 1 800 | 1 900 | (100) | (5.6) |
| Indirect labour | 3 600 | 3 600 | — | — |
| Supplies | 360 | 480 | (120) | (33.3) |
| Power | 3 400 | 3 100 | 300 | 8.8 |
| Repairs | 1 600 | 1 200 | 400 | 25.0 |
| TOTAL EXPENSES | 29 360 | 31 380 | (2 020) | (6.9) |

Nobody really expects that all of the actual figures will be right on budget. If they were, we'd probably be very suspicious of them. So what is a significant variance? Three essential pieces of information may be assessed in considering significance.

1. The absolute amount in dollars shown by the variance. Even if the variance is large in relation to the budgeted figure, there is not much point in investigating a $50 variance. It will cost much more than that to track it down. Even a $100 variance is seldom worth investigating.

2. The relative amount in terms of percentage. The fact that the performance report in Figure 11.1 shows a column for the variance percentage indicates that this company considers the relative size of the variance to be important. The figure is simply the variance as a percentage of the budgeted amount. Many companies have policies about the tolerable variance percentages. They may decide, for instance, that all variances over 5

per cent must be investigated unless the absolute amount is less than $100.

3   The pattern of the variances. Even a comparatively small variance can cause concern if it is always unfavorable. Over time this may mean that the expense is costing much more than has been allowed for in the budget.

Applying these rules to the example in Figure 11.1, we can see that some of the variances are very significant. It is significant that production is substantially below budget. The explanation for this may be quite simple. There may have been a major breakdown or an industrial dispute. However, if there is no obvious explanation of this kind, close investigation will be necessary. This unfavorable production variance is significant for another reason. One would expect that lower production would lead to lower expenses, particularly where they should be variable with the level of production. We could reasonably expect, for example, that there would be no need for overtime, that power requirements and repairs will be down.

One would expect that normal labour costs would be regular and close to the budget figures, apart from unanticipated wage rises. By the 5 per cent rule this variance is not significant. However, although no overtime was budgeted, $1600 has been spent on overtime in a month when production was below budget. There must be some explanation for this. Perhaps there was a major breakdown and this led to the necessity to work overtime to catch up. If this is so, why is the repairs expense below budget? It appears possible that unnecessary overtime has been worked. An immediate investigation would be launched to see who authorised the overtime and why.

The actual variance in maintenance expenses is only $100 so it is probably not worth further investigation. There is no variance in indirect labour (supervision salaries). Supplies, in our example, consist of lubricants, cleaning materials, brooms and other small items. They are often the target of pilferers or are used wastefully. In this case the absolute variance between budgeted and actual cost is not large, but in relative terms it is significant. It would be worthwhile here to investigate the supplies situation to see where the over-use has occurred and perhaps to review the control procedures on use of supplies.

Power is below budget, as it should be when production is below budget. Repairs are well below budget, which is worth investigating, although this is not necessarily unusual. It may be that on the first day of the next month a major repair is necessary which will blow not only this favourable variance but the whole of next month's budget.

Taken overall the only reasons for concern seem to be the overtime which was not budgeted for at all; the over-use of supplies; and the overall variance that caused costs to be 6.9 per cent higher than budget. This overall figure is not quite into Valium territory but is in the region of strong coffee, a Panadol and a lie-down. If the manager is to be judged according to the ability to control costs, then the successful manager must do just that.

## Engineered Expenses

Some expenses arise automatically out of the level of activity, others arise at the discretion of management. Engineered expenses are those where there is a strong causal relationship between the level of production and the amount of expense. Raw material used is a good example. The manufacture of a product causes the use of the raw material. The engineers will decide how the article is to be produced and once this is decided they can estimate the quantity of raw material required to produce one unit of product. This may be done by test runs. Once this usage per unit of product is determined, there should not be any significant variations in the amount of raw material used per unit unless the production methods are changed or there is a different grade of material used. If there is significant variation it will probably be due to inefficiencies or wastage. Other engineered expenses include direct labour, where usage may be determined by time and motion studies; and scheduled maintenance.

## Managed Expenses

Managed expenses (or discretionary expenses) are expenses where there is little causal relationship between the production level and the expense. A good example of a managed expense is advertising. Clearly there is a link between production levels and advertising but it is not directly and immediately causal. The results of advertising may make an impact on production some time after the advertising costs are expended. Because the links are not strong, some accountants refer to managed expenses as discretionary expenses, which creates the feeling that the company can choose to spend the money or not spend it. In the long term, of course, this is not true. A decision not to advertise now may lead to loss of market share and disaster in some future period. The trouble is that you just can't prove the effect of the managed expense.

Because of the stronger links with production and the greater surety of outcome, the reporting of engineered expenses is often more formal and tightly quantified. Managed expenses are often reported less formally.

## Standard Costing Systems

Many businesses, particularly those in manufacturing, use **standard costing systems**. A standard costing system allows for tighter control and investigation of variances in engineered expenses, particularly raw materials, direct labour and manufacturing overheads. Standard costing allows the manager to more accurately investigate variances in engineered expenses to explain why the variances have occurred. The standard costing system produces performance reports but the system has built in mechanisms to aid closer investigation of variances.

The fundamental difference between standard costing and the earlier performance reports is that those earlier ones were based on historical costs. Standard costing reports are based on expected cost so the setting of realistic standards is an important part of the process.

Standard costing relies on the comparison of actual with expected results. So the expectations have to be quantified and regularly updated. The validity of a standard costing system relies on the relevance and reliability of the standards set. If the standards are set unrealistically then the system will not operate as it should. Standards can be set at three different levels.

- **Ideal standards** assume perfect performance by machines and employees, no wastage or spoilage of material and complete control of all inputs; they are probably not achievable.
- **Optimal standards** are achievable standards based on realistic peak performance by machines and employees.
- **Expected standards** are very realistic, allowing for normal wastage levels, machine downtime, average employee performance and idle time.

It is sometimes argued that ideal standards motivate employees because workers will strive to reach them, thus exceeding their usual efforts. However, it is unlikely that employees will not see clearly what is going on and make little effort to achieve them. Often ideal standards lose their credibility very quickly, particularly in the Australian work environment. Expected standards may be too easily achieved and require little effort so that there is little motivation to achieve improvement. They can also cause problems if they are used by unions in collective bargaining situations. The union may claim that the standards set by the employer have been exceeded and argue for pay increases based on productivity gains. All in all then, optimal standards are usually favoured.

Once the standards are set they must be continually updated as prices, conditions and technology change.

Standards must be set for materials, direct labour and overheads. Once they are set and found to be working well the tendency will be to adjust them regularly, but only for inflation and changes in specifications and procedures.

To illustrate the standard setting process, we will use the example of a cheap laminate-topped bench with metal legs, the type often inflicted upon students in tertiary institutions. We will assume that the management has the sense to use optimal standards. Material, labour and overheads must be considered separately.

First we shall consider materials. Decisions have to be made about the type and quality of materials to be used. Our bench consists of tubular steel legs and top frame, laminated chipboard top, screws to join them together and some paint. Different weights and thicknesses of tubular steel would be tested to see which is the cheapest material adequate for the purpose. The same applies to the thickness of the material for the top. This work will be done by the product designers and product engineers.

The design department will draw up specifications, the production department will estimate wastage. Perhaps there will be a trade-off considered. If there is a thinner, cheaper material used for the top, wastage factors may be higher. A decision may be taken based on minimising overall costs. The purchasing department will provide prices and make supply contracts.

Next we shall look at labour. The major decisions are about the type of labour required and the time that it should take to complete each process in the production. Production of the bench consists of four major tasks.

1   The tubular steel has to be cut to length with a power hacksaw; this can be done by comparatively unskilled labour.

2   The pieces of frame have to be welded together, which requires a qualified welder whose pay rate will be higher than that of an unskilled worker.

3   The constructed frame must be sprayed with paint, requiring no special skills.

4   The frame must be joined to the top, which can also be done under supervision by unskilled labour.

Each of the tasks will be assessed by work studies to set standard times for their completion. The personnel department will supply details of the wage rates that must be paid to each type of worker.

The last thing to be considered is overheads. Decisions will be made on the amount of additional fixed overhead and the variable overheads likely to be incurred, and an absorption rate for overhead will be struck. The absorption rate is obtained by dividing the budgeted overheads for the period by some logical unit, like direct labour hours planned. It will be assumed that as direct labour hours are worked, overheads will occur in proportion.

In this way, the standard material usage and material cost per unit of product (probably per desk in our example) will be set. So will the standard labour time and cost per unit of product, and the standard overhead per unit.

For our purposes here we will assume that the standard materials per desk consist of:

> 8 metres of tubular steel at $2.50 per metre
> 1 laminated top at $5
> 10 screws at 10 cents each
> 200 ml of paint at $4 per litre

The standard labour cost consists of 1.5 hours of labour at $8 per hour. The overhead absorption rate is $4 per direct labour hour.

The assumption will be, then, that if 1000 desks are produced, the usage and cost of materials, labour and overhead will be 1000 times each of these figures. That is, we should have used:

> 8000 metres of tubular steel costing $20 000
> 1000 laminated tops costing $5000
> 10 000 screws costing $1000
> 200 litres of paint costing $800
> 1500 hours of direct labour costing $12 000
>
> Overheads should have cost $6000 (1500 hours x $4).

There is one thing you can be sure of: at the end of the period the actual figures will not be the same as this. A count of the stocks, and the analysis of costs, indicates that in actual fact we used:

> 8400 metres of tubular steel costing $21 840
> 1040 laminated tops costing $5096
> 9600 screws costing $1056
> 180 litres of paint costing $720
> 1400 hours of labour costing $11 900
>
> Overheads were $6500.

A simple performance report of the type used earlier would indicate that a problem exists. The report is shown in Figure 11.2 (F and U stand for favourable and unfavorable). However, there is not enough information here. All that this performance report tells us is that there is a problem in the materials area somewhere; there is no problem with labour; we have overspent on overheads; and that overall we have a problem. By carrying out a full analysis of variances using the standard costing system, we can discover much more than this.

**Figure 11.2**
**CHEAP BENCH DEPARTMENT**
**Performance Report**

| Production (units) | Budget | Actual | Variance |
|---|---|---|---|
|  | 1 000 | 1 000 | — |
| *Expenses* | | | |
| Material | $26 800 | 28 712 | (1 912) U |
| Direct labour | 12 000 | 11 900 | 100 F |
| Overheads | 6 000 | 6 500 | (500) U |
| TOTAL EXPENSES | $44 800 | $47 112 | $(2 312) U |

## Material Price Variance and Material Usage Variance

First, of all we will analyse what has happened with the raw materials. The analysis of materials variances using standard costs will enable us to find two separate variances for each class of material. One is a price variance, which shows how much of the variance from budget to actual is due to changes in price of the material; and the other is a usage variance (sometimes referred to as quantity variance), which shows how much of the variance is due to wastage or loss of material.

We need to separate these variances because price variances are the responsibility of the purchasing department and usage variances are the responsibility of the production department.

The material price variances can be expressed as the difference between the quantity purchased at the actual price paid and the amount that the quantity purchased would have cost at its standard price. As a formula:

Material price variance = (AP x AQ) − (SP x AQ)

where AP = the actual price paid per unit
AQ = the actual quantity purchased
SP = the standard price per unit

(AP x AQ) is therefore the total amount actually paid.

In the case of the tubular steel:

Material price variance = (AP x AQ) − (SP x AQ)
= $(21 840) − $(2.50 x 8400)
= $840 *U*

The variance is unfavorable because actual cost is greater than standard cost.

For the laminated tops:

Material price variance = (AP x AQ) − (SP x AQ)
= $(5096) − $(5 x 1040)
= $104 *F*

This variance is favourable because actual cost is less than standard cost.

For the screws:

Material price variance = (AP x AQ) − (SP x AQ)
= $(1056) − $(0.10 x 9600)
= $96 *U*

This variance is unfavorable because actual cost is greater than standard cost.

For the paint:

Material price variance = (AP x AQ) − (SP x AQ)
= $(720) − $(4 x 180)
= 0

There is no price variance for the paint.

Now that we have found the price variances for each of the materials, we will calculate the materials usage variances. These variances could be described as the difference between the actual quantity of material used and the quantity that should have been used if the standards had been adhered to, valued at the standard price. The difference is valued at standard price, because if actual price was used the price variance on those units would be double-counted. As a formula:

In the case of the tubular steel:

$$\begin{aligned}\text{Material usage variance} &= (AQ \times SP) - (SQ \times SP) \\ &= \$(8400 \times 2.50) - \$(8000 \times 2.50) \\ &= \$1000 \ U\end{aligned}$$

This is an unfavorable variance because the actual usage is greater than the standard usage. It consists of the 400 extra metres of steel we used at their standard cost of $2.50 per metre.

For the laminated tops:

$$\begin{aligned}\text{Material usage variance} &= (AQ \times SP) - (SQ \times SP) \\ &= \$(1040 \times 5) - \$(1000 \times 5) \\ &= \$200 \ U\end{aligned}$$

This is an unfavorable variance because the actual usage is greater than the standard usage. This usage variance consists of the forty extra tops we used at their standard price of $5 each.

For the screws:

$$\begin{aligned}\text{Material usage variance} &= (AQ \times SP) - (SQ \times SP) \\ &= \$(9600 \times 0.10) - \$(10\,000 \times 0.10) \\ &= \$40 \ F\end{aligned}$$

This variance is favourable because actual usage is less than standard usage. The variance consists of using 400 less screws than expected at 10 cents each. This is strange because each bench is supposed to have ten screws. What it means is that our employees are not putting in the full number of screws every time. Some benches are likely to be returned or rejected as a result of this. It requires immediate attention.

For the paint:

$$\begin{aligned}\text{Material usage variance} &= (AQ \times SP) - (SQ \times SP) \\ &= \$(180 \times 4) - \$(200 \times 4) \\ &= \$80 \; F\end{aligned}$$

This is a favourable variance because actual usage is less than expected under the standard. It consists of using 20 litres less paint than expected, at $4 per litre. This may be a good thing or a bad thing depending upon the reason.

Figure 11.3 summarises the materials variances.

**Figure 11.3**

| Materials | Price variance | Usage variance | Total variance |
|---|---|---|---|
| Tubular steel | $840 U | 1000 U | 1840 U |
| Laminated tops | 104 F | 200 U | 96 U |
| Screws | 96 U | 40 F | 56 U |
| Paint | 0 | 80 F | 80 F |
| TOTAL | $832 U | $1080 U | $1912 U |

The total materials variance is the same as that shown in the performance report but we now have several pieces of additional information.

We know that:

- We are paying more than expected for the tubular steel and the screws. This is not the production department's problem. It should be referred to the purchasing department.

- The purchasing department is managing to buy the laminated tops at a cheaper price than expected. Perhaps this is related to the unfavorable usage variance. If the cheaper tops are of lower quality there may be more wastage as they become damaged during attachment to the frames.

- We seem to be using a lot more steel than we expected. This could be due to wastage. Perhaps the lengths being bought in do not cut into an exact number of component parts so there is a wasted piece at the end of every length. Perhaps some steel is being stolen or used on personal work. It should not be a quality problem because it is being bought at a higher price than expected.

- Benches are obviously going out with less than the full complement of screws.

- We are not using as much paint as expected. If this is due to an over-statement of the quantity required in the standard or is due to care by the employees, this is a good trend. However, it may be due to insufficient paint being used which could lead to rusting of the bench legs. It may well be that the painters are not painting the top of the frames under the bench top.

Fortified by all of this information and a Johnny Walker or two, we will now analyse the direct labour situation. The analysis of direct labour variances using standard costs will enable us to calculate two separate variances for direct labour. These are:

- a rate variance (similar to the material price variance), which is due to the hourly wage rate not being what the standard predicted; and

- an efficiency variance (similar to the material usage variance), which is due to the labour hours used being not equal to those allowed for in the standard.

Again, it is important to separate the effects of these two differences. The rate variance is the responsibility of the personnel department and the efficiency variance is the production department's problem.

The labour rate variance can be expressed as the difference between the actual hours worked at the actual rate and the amount that it would have cost if that number of hours had been worked at the standard rate.

As a formula:

Labour rate variance = (AR x AQ) − (SR x AQ)

where AR = the actual labour rate per hour
AQ = the actual hours worked
SR = the standard labour rate per hour

(AR x AQ) will equal the total wages paid.

For the manufacture of the 1000 cheap benches:

Labour rate variance = (AR x AQ) − (SR x AQ)
= $(11 900) − $(8 x 1400)
= $700 *U*

This is an unfavorable variance because the actual hours worked have cost more in wages than they would have under the standard rate. The $700 unfavorable rate variance represents an extra 50 cents in wages for each of the 1400 hours worked.

The labour efficiency variance represents the difference between the total number of hours that it should have taken to produce the output and the number of hours that it actually took. It is calculated at the standard hourly labour rate to avoid double counting the rate variance in those hours. As a formula:

Labour efficiency variance = (AQ x SR) − (SQ x SR)

where AQ = the actual hours worked
SR = the standard labour rate per hour
SQ = the standard hours that should have been worked

For the manufacture of the 1000 benches:

Labour efficiency variance = R(1400 x 8) − R(1500 x 8)
= $800 F

This is a favourable variance because the actual cost is less than the standard cost. The variance represents 100 hours less than expected being worked, at the standard rate of $8 per hour.

So we now have much more information about the labour costs. In the simple performance report, all we knew was that there was a $100 favourable variance for labour cost. Now we know that this difference in labour cost actually consists of the net result of two relatively large variances. There is a serious rate variance due to labour costing fifty cents per hour more than was expected. (This is the personnel department's problem.) There is also a large favourable variance in labour efficiency.

One possible explanation of this combination of variances is that the workers hired to do the job are more skilled than was really required, hence their higher hourly rates and faster work. However, in the light of the screw usage situation, the problem may be an over-zealous supervisor who is driving the workers along so fast that the job is not being done properly.

As you can see, once again the use of standard costing gives us much more information than we could get from the simple performance report.

The analysis of standard costs will enable us to calculate two separate variances for variable overheads:

- a spending variance which results from overheads costing more than expected; and
- an efficiency variance which results from the number of direct labour hours worked being not the same as that anticipated when the standards were set.

The variable overhead spending variance can be expressed as the difference between the actual amount spent on variable overheads and the amount that should have been spent for the actual number of hours worked.

As a formula:

> Variable overhead
> spending variance = $(AQ \times AOR) - (AQ \times SOR)$
>
> where AQ = the actual direct labour hours worked
> AOR = the actual overhead rate per hour
> SOR = the standard overhead absorption rate
>
> (AQ x AOR) will equal the actual amount spent on variable overhead.

In the case of our 1000 benches:

> Variable overhead
> spending variance = $(6500) - (1400 \times 4)$
> = $900 *U*

This variance is unfavourable because the actual amount spent on variable overhead is more than it should have been under the standard rate set down.

The variable overhead efficiency variance can be expressed as the difference between the direct labour hours actually worked and the direct labour hours expected to be required, valued at the standard rate of variable overhead expected per hour. As a formula:

Variable overhead
efficiency variance = (AQ x SOR) − (SQ x SOR)

where AQ = the actual direct labour hours worked
SOR = the standard overhead absorption rate
SQ = the standard direct labour hours that should have been required

In the case of our benches:

Variable overhead
efficiency variance = (AQ x SOR) − (SQ x SOR)
= $(1400 x 4) − $(1500 x 4)
= $400 F

This variance is favourable because the actual cost is less than the standard cost expected.

From the simple performance report shown in Figure 11.2, we knew only that there was a $500 unfavourable overhead variance taken overall. Now we know that this total variance consists of a $900 unfavourable spending variance (much more than was expected has been spent on overheads); and a $400 favourable efficiency variance which is due to less hours being worked than was anticipated. Immediate steps should be taken to investigate which specific overheads are causing the problem of over-spending and why.

As we have seen from what may appear a somewhat complex and protracted example, standard cost analysis can be used to provide lots of valuable information that we did not have before. In practical terms there is virtually no limit to it. Just think how complex this analysis becomes, however, if it is applied in a manufacturing situation where there are a thousand different raw materials and components all with their own individual price and usage variances, fifty different classes of labour each with its own rate and efficiency variance, and hundreds of different groups of overheads.

It is easy to produce the information, and computerised systems can churn it out relentlessly, destroying forest after forest. But is it all worth it? Can we really use all of that information? Is the cost of producing it justified? Do all of the managers receiving the information really understand what they are looking at? Probably not.

Back in the days when I was young and enthusiastic I had a naive belief that all the world shared my enthusiasm for information. On one occasion I spent four weeks of my spare waking moments producing a report for the Managing Director into ways that costs could be saved in the production processes. It involved hundreds of ideas gleaned from my days at university, lovingly applied to the firm's special problems. This was my baby, my creation. I had it bound in a bright, striking cover. I could hardly wait for the following Monday morning to come around so that I could hand it to the chief. All weekend I dreamed of the praise that would be heaped on me as my suggestions were implemented and the company leapt to new horizons of profitability.

Monday morning came and I handed it to the Managing Director personally and held my breath.

'Nice cover', he grunted and stuck it in his drawer. I never heard of it again.

# 12

# Revenue Centres: Little Goldmines or . . .?

In the best of organised situations, things can often go wrong and sometimes some little area still escapes the ravages of cost cutting managers. For example, it is true that in 1803 the British Parliament created a public service job for a man to stand on top of the white cliffs at Dover with a telescope and a bell. The idea was that if he saw Napoleon coming he would ring the bell. Napoleon died in 1821. The job was abolished in 1945.

## Responsibilities of the Revenue Centre Manager

In the cost centre we saw that the manager's prime responsibility was to operate within the parameters set by the budget and the standards. In a revenue centre the major requirement is to attain the budgeted levels of revenue. Most revenue centres are sales departments. As well as reaching budgeted sales figures, typically they also have to exercise control over marketing costs. However, the major problem is achieving the required revenue level. The key factors are the sales volume of product; the product selling price; and the sales mix of the products sold.

We saw in chapter 7 that the starting point for the year's planning is the sales budget. So in controlling revenue it is important to know at all times whether the planned volume of sales has been achieved. Many organisations subdivide their sales into geographic regions such as states, or by marketing method such as retail and wholesale. Reports on sales progress are usually set out in detail so that regional problems or market segment problems are easily identified. The sales report in Figure 12.1 is typical of this kind of report.

In this report we can see that the totals indicate quite a successful year so far with actual results being better than budget both in May and for the year to date.

**Figure 12.1**
**GASPERS LTD**
**Sales Report for May 19--**

|  | LAST MONTH |  | YEAR TO DATE |  |
|---|---|---|---|---|
| Region | Actual | Budget | Actual | Budget |
|  | $ | $ | $ | $ |
| Northern | 210 000 | 160 000 | 940 000 | 800 000 |
| NSW | 320 000 | 280 000 | 1 310 000 | 1 250 000 |
| Victoria | 260 000 | 255 000 | 1 550 000 | 1 700 000 |
| Western | 140 000 | 180 000 | 640 000 | 850 000 |
| TOTAL | 930 000 | 875 000 | 4 440 000 | 4 600 000 |

However, closer analysis of the figures by region indicates that problems certainly exist. Both Victoria and the Western region are well below budget expectations. Western is in fact about 25 per cent under budget. This is a situation requiring more detailed analysis within the region's figures. Perhaps the problem is in one territory or one type of sale or perhaps there are local reasons such as increased competition in that region. It is not possible to start solving the problem until it is specifically identified. It's probably not usually as simple as this problem at Macho Menswear.

At Macho Menswear the general manager couldn't understand why one of his salesmen, Barkly, had such poor results.

'Look, Barkly,' he said eventually, 'your figures are so bad that unless they improve in the next month, we'll have to let you go.'

'I know they're not good,' Barkly said, 'but can you let me have some advice about how I might improve?'

'Well there is one thing you could try', the manager said. 'Go through the dictionary and look for really powerful words. When you find them, memorise them, and build them into your sales talk.'

The next month Barkly's sales were the best the manager had ever seen from anybody, so he called Barkly back into the office.

'Congratulations,' he said, 'you've made record figures. I've never seen such a result. How did you do it?'

'Well' Barkly replied, 'I did what you said. Went through the dictionary for hours and eventually found a really powerful word.'

'What was it?'

'Fantastic.'

'Fantastic, eh. Yes, that's a good strong word. How did you build that into the sales talk?'

'Well one of my first customers was a woman with a little boy. She told me that she had sent him to a very exclusive private school. I said, "Fantastic!" Then she told me that he was the top student in his class. I said, "Fantastic!" She said that not only was he a great scholar but he was also a brilliant sportsman. He was a future league footballer, a regular Bradman with the bat, and a top athlete and swimmer. I said, "Fantastic!" She bought three pairs of grey trousers, four pairs of shorts, five shirts and five sets of underwear.'

'The next customer was a middle-aged gentleman who told me he played golf down at the Royal Melbourne Golf Club. I said, "Fantastic!" He said he was playing with the club pro and beat him by five strokes. I said, "Fantastic!" He said that the thing that won it for him was a string of birdies. I said, "Fantastic!" He said that he might be a contender for a place in the state amateur team. I said, "Fantastic!" He bought three pairs of sports trousers, a jacket and six shirts. And that's gone on all week. The more the customers boast, the more I go on saying, "Fantastic!" They just buy and buy.'

'That's great, Barkly,' the manager said, 'but just out of interest, what did you say to these people when they were boasting, before you read the dictionary and discovered "Fantastic"?'

'Oh, I just used to say, "Ah, bull dust!" '

## The Problem of Maintaining Sales Revenue

The second key factor in achieving the required revenue level is selling price. There are many reasons why actual selling price may be quite different from planned selling price. The economic conditions at the time may lead to price cutting, or new competitors may come into the market. New marketing strategies may be developed or it may be company policy to allow salespeople latitude in quoting prices.

As we have already seen, the critical factor in generating profit is the creation of contribution margin, that is, the difference between selling price and variable cost. This is so important that we considered in detail the many ways in which variable cost may be tightly controlled. Clearly, though, the contribution margin is just as greatly affected by variations in selling price.

If an article sells for $10 and has a variable cost of $3, the contribution margin will drop from $7 to $6.50 when the variable cost increases by 50 cents. This would represent a major cost escalation of nearly 17 per cent. However, a price cut of only 5 per cent (50 cents) would have the same effect. The contribution margin would decrease by the same amount. Therefore it is important to be very careful when undertaking price cutting. You must be very sure that by cutting the price, sales will expand sufficiently to more than cover that lost contribution margin.

An assessment may be made of this situation in advance. We may find, for instance, that our estimates are as shown below for burples, which have a variable cost of $7:

|  | Selling price | Likely sales level |
|---|---|---|
| Current position | $10 | 5 000 |
| Propositions |  |  |
| (a) Drop selling price to $9.50 | $9.50 | 5 500 |
| (b) Drop selling price to $9 | $9 | 6 000 |
| (c) Drop selling price to $8 | $8 | 10 000 |

Because variable costs and fixed costs remain consistent, the most profitable situation is the one where contribution margin is maximised. We can show this in a table:

| Selling price per unit | Variable cost per unit | Contribution margin per unit | Sales level estimated | Total CM |
|---|---|---|---|---|
| $10.00 | $7.00 | $3.00 | 5 000 | $15 000 |
| 9.50 | 7.00 | 2.50 | 6 200 | $15 500 |
| 9.00 | 7.00 | 2.00 | 7 200 | $14 400 |
| 8.00 | 7.00 | 1.00 | 10 000 | $10 000 |

The most profitable strategy appears to be to drop the price to $9.50, and further price cutting is counter-productive even though sales are doubled when the price is dropped to $8. Note, however, that in order to earn that extra $500 in contribution margin, the sales have to be increased from 5000 units to 6200 units, an increase in sales level of 24 per cent. It is this sort of problem that leads to the general belief that price cutting is a dangerous activity unless you can maintain contribution margin per unit by buying or making the article more cheaply.

Even when price cutting is used to build market share, it is dangerous because your newly-gained customers may expect the price cuts to be permanent, and you may also damage your brand image by making people perceive it as a cheap brand.

Because selling price is so sensitive, the accounting system must provide information on actual selling prices compared with planned selling prices.

Different sales lines have different contribution margins and, as we have seen, maximising total contribution margin is what making a profit is all about. So changes in the sales mix, the proportions of various products sold, can affect profitability even if sales revenue is the same. Take the Flipper Company Ltd, for example, which sells three products. Last year the sales data were:

|  | Per unit ||| Sales | Total | Total |
|  | SP | VC | CM | (units) | sales | CM |
| --- | --- | --- | --- | --- | --- | --- |
| Whipper | $5.00 | 3.00 | 2.00 | 100 000 | $500 000 | $200 000 |
| Slipper | 5.00 | 1.00 | 4.00 | 120 000 | 600 000 | $480 000 |
| Kipper | 7.00 | 5.00 | 2.00 | 200 000 | 1 400 000 | $400 000 |
|  |  |  |  | 420 000 | 2 500 000 | $1 080 000 |

This year the sales revenue has grown from $2 500 000 to $2 810 000, a growth of over 12 per cent. There has been no change in selling prices but profits appear to be down. An analysis shows that the problem is purely one of change in sales mix.

|  | Per unit ||| Sales | Total | Total |
|  | SP | VC | CM | (units) | sales | CM |
| --- | --- | --- | --- | --- | --- | --- |
| Whipper | $5.00 | 3.00 | 2.00 | 100 000 | $500 000 | $200 000 |
| Slipper | 5.00 | 1.00 | 4.00 | 70 000 | 350 000 | $280 000 |
| Kipper | 7.00 | 5.00 | 2.00 | 280 000 | 1 960 000 | $560 000 |
|  |  |  |  | 450 000 | 2 810 000 | $1 040 000 |

Despite the $310 000 increase in sales revenue, there has been a $40 000 drop in contribution margin earned, which also means a $40 000 drop in profit. The sole reason is the decrease in sales of Slipper product which has the highest contribution margin per unit. The message from this is that sales managers should concentrate on maintaining contribution margin rather than revenue alone and this means keeping a close eye on the sales mix.

This also means, of course, that the accounting system must provide the manager with information about the actual sales mix compared with planned sales mix and the impact of the differences on profitability. Although the specific procedures adopted for variance analysis in revenue centres may vary from firm to firm, the most commonly used variances reported to sales managers are:

1. price variance, which will indicate whether products are being sold at discount prices not planned for originally;
2. sales volume variance, which will indicate whether sales levels are different from what was expected;
3. contribution margin mix variance, which will indicate whether and how contribution margin has been affected by unexpected changes in sales volume of their product.

## Sales Price Variance

The price variance is the difference between the expected revenue and actual revenue which has arisen as a result of unexpected price variations. This may result from changes in market conditions such as competition, and in the economy. It may also result from sales strategies such as cut-price sales and attempts at market expansion. This variance may be calculated for each product separately. The actual number of units sold is multiplied by the difference between actual and budgeted price. That is:

$$\text{Price variance} = AQ \times (AP - BP)$$

where AQ = the actual quantity of units sold
AP = the actual selling price
BP = the budgeted selling price.

So if we expected to sell our product at $25 per unit and we have sold 15 000 of them at $23.50, the price variance is:

```
Price variance = AQ x (AP − BP)
              = 15 000 x ($25 − $23.50)
              = $22 500 U
```

It is an unfavorable price variance because the actual figure is below the budgeted figure.

It is likely that some products will have favourable price variances and some unfavorable price variances. Where there are many different products, the detail in reports received will depend upon the manager's level. Higher-level managers may receive summaries according to product line or department. Lower-level managers may receive very detailed reports about their groups of products.

The price variance shown here is substantial and it indicates that price cutting has reduced revenue by $22 500 in this period. Other information will be sought by the manager concerned to determine whether this is the result of marketing problems or external factors in the market.

### The Sales Volume Variance

The sales volume variance is calculated in much the same way as the quantity variance in a standard cost system. It is the difference in total revenue caused by differences in the number of units sold. Again, this will normally be calculated for each product or product line. As a formula:

```
Volume variance = (AQ − BQ) x BP

where AQ = the actual quantity of units sold
      BQ = the budgeted sales of the product in units
      BP = the budgeted selling price for the product per unit
```

If the budget indicated that we expected to sell 1500 units of product at $18 each and we find that we have sold 1150 units, we can calculate the volume variance in sales dollars:

$$\begin{aligned}\text{Volume variance} &= (AQ - BQ) \times BP \\ &= (\$1150 - \$1500) \times \$18 \\ &= \$6300 \ U\end{aligned}$$

The lower level of sales than expected has cost us $6300 in sales revenue.

Suppose that you have been told that budgeted sales revenue for drapples for the quarter was expected to be $108 000 but it is only $104 500. The total variance in sales revenue is not serious but we look more closely at it anyway. We find in fact that the detailed sales budget anticipated sales of 9 000 units at $12 each. In fact, what we have is sales of 9 500 units at $11 each. We can now separate the effects of price and volume variances on sales revenue:

$$\begin{aligned}\text{Price variance} &= AQ \times (AP - BP) \\ &= 9500 \times (\$11 - \$12) \\ &= \$9500 \ U\end{aligned}$$

$$\begin{aligned}\text{Volume variance} &= (AQ - BQ) \times BP \\ &= (9500 - 9000) \times \$12 \\ &= \$6000 \ F\end{aligned}$$

So, in fact, the difference in sales revenue of $3500 is due to the net effect of an unfavorable price variance of $9500 and a favourable volume variance of $6000. We are selling more units but at a lower price. Significantly, the net effect is lower revenue and almost certainly lower profitability. Having separated the effects of price and volume, we have much more valuable information than when we only knew that sales revenue was $3500 below budget.

### The Contribution Margin Mix Variance

The contribution margin mix variance is designed to tell us the net effect that changes in sales mix have had on total contribution margin. The calculation is made at budgeted prices to eliminate any effect of price changes, which will be part of the price variance. A full analysis of budgeted contribution margin is compared with actual contribution margin.

Suppose that Flipper Company Ltd, which we used as an example in looking at sales mix, had used last year's figures as the budget figures for this year. (Not a recommended practice but a reasonably common one.) The budgeted contribution margin figures would be the same as last year's actual figures.

The formula for the contribution margin mix variance is:

Contribution margin mix variance = the total for all products of (AQ − BQ) × BCM

where AQ = the actual quantity of units sold
BQ = the budgeted sales of the product in units
BCM = the budgeted contribution margin per unit

For Flipper Company Ltd:

|  | AQ (units) | BQ (units) | AQ-BQ | CM per unit | Variance |
|---|---|---|---|---|---|
| Whipper | 100 000 | 100 000 | — | $2.00 | — |
| Slipper | 70 000 | 120 000 | (50 000) | 4.00 | $(200 000) |
| Kipper | 280 000 | 200 000 | 80 000 | 2.00 | $160 000 |
|  | 450 000 | 420 000 |  |  | $(40 000) |

We now have a full analysis of the sales situation and we can see just how serious the effects are of a change in sales mix from Slipper to Kipper. If the products are similar in nature, we would be anxious to re-establish higher sales levels of Slipper even at the expense of Kipper.

## Importance of Market Share

Apart from controlling costs and revenue in the revenue centre, the manager has a number of other concerns. As we have already stressed, market share is very important. It is usually calculated on dollar sales data, so it may be affected by price variations. The data for the total market is usually obtained either from industry associations or from government statistics. Many firms produce market share reports, monthly, quarterly or annually. A simple report may be along the lines of that shown in Figure 12.2.

**Figure 12.2**
**COMFY FOOTWEAR LTD (%)**
**Market Share Report**

| Product line | Current quarter | Last quarter | Last year | Objectives |
|---|---|---|---|---|
| Women's shoes | 7 | 7 | 8 | 6 |
| Men's shoes | 3 | 3 | 4 | 3 |
| Sports shoes | 18 | 16 | 15 | 20 |
| Children's shoes | 22 | 21 | 19 | 25 |

This market share report shows that the company is moving well towards its objectives, expanding its market share of the sports and children's segments. The importance of trends in these figures may lead to data being given for the last four quarters. The objectives will have been established in the profit plan.

## The Sales Manager and Debtors Turnover and Stock Turn

Although the debtors' turnover rate is primarily the concern of the credit manager, it is also of interest to the sales manager. Control must be exercised over the likelihood of slow-paying or non-paying customers. It is much better if the sales manager and credit manager work together on this. Increasingly these days, sales representatives and sales departments are made responsible for their own collection of outstanding accounts. Bad debts may be charged back against the sales department.

Stock turnover for the various product lines and individual products must be continually monitored to avoid build up and over-stocking of lines. Fast moving lines must be carefully watched to avoid stock-outs.

## The Backlog of Orders Report

The backlog of orders represents orders that have been received but have not yet been supplied. Sometimes this is separated into 'overdue' for orders past the due date of delivery and 'not yet due' for forward orders not yet due to be supplied.

## Advertising Expenditure

Most revenue centre managers will have some responsibility for advertising expenditure. Measuring the effectiveness of advertising is very difficult and this often leads to conflict with accountants. The effectiveness of raw material costs, direct labour, electricity and administrative expenses can easily be seen.

The effects of advertising and promotion are not as obvious. There may be weeks between the time of the advertisement and the gaining of sales revenue. Sometimes advertising is done to generate public awareness of the company and its products so that there is no direct revenue result.

Attempts at measuring the effects of advertising often centre on asking customers where they heard about the product, or surveying people to find out if they have heard of the product. It is generally agreed these days that this type of research is not very effective. A certain amount of blind faith is required of managers who institute advertising campaigns, with an awareness that in the short run at least they may never know how effective the campaign was.

## Sales Representatives' Performance Reports

We have already seen how significant the price, volume and contribution margin mix variances are in controlling the revenue centre. To a certain extent these variances are controlled by the individual sales representatives, so a report showing variances for each sales representative will be of value to the manager. It will act as a check on volume against quota, an indication of the representative's tendency to cut prices to make sales, and will indicate whether the sales representative places sufficient emphasis on products which make the best contribution to profit.

This may lead to the preparation of a sales representative's performance summary as shown in Figure 12.3.

**Figure 12.3**
**Sales Representatives' Performance Summary**

|  | \multicolumn{6}{c|}{CURRENT MONTH} | \multicolumn{2}{c}{YEAR TO DATE} |
|---|---|---|---|---|---|---|---|---|
|  | Actual sales | Quota | Price variance | Volume variance | CM mix variance | Commission earned | Quota | Total variance |
|  | $ | $ | $ | $ | $ | $ | $ | $ |
| Brown | 18 300 | 20 000 | 200 F | 1 900 U | 400 F | 1 100 | 90 000 | 5 200 U |
| Green | 20 100 | 20 000 | 120 U | 220 F | 100 F | 1 200 | 90 000 | 1 000 F |
| Black | 16 000 | 20 000 | 2 200 U | 1 800 U | 700 U | 150 | 90 000 | 20 000 U |
| White | 24 000 | 20 000 | 200 U | 4 200 F | 2 200 F | 3 100 | 90 000 | 18 600 F |
|  | 78 400 | 80 000 | 2 320 U | 720 F | 2 000 F | 5 550 | 360 000 | 5 600 U |

The performance summary gives quite a good picture of each salesperson's performance.

Brown is below quota and has a small favourable price variance and a considerable unfavorable volume variance. This may indicate that Brown is trying too hard to get the set prices or even a little more. This is adversely affecting total sales. Brown could be counseled to be a little more flexible in selling terms as the variance from quota is becoming serious.

Green is almost right on track. Not an exciting performance, but a reliable one.

Black has a disastrous performance. Not only has Black seriously failed to meet quota, but this has occurred even with price cutting, as the unfavorable price variance indicates. Unless there is some mitigating circumstance for all this, we would probably terminate Black's employment.

White is the star sales representative with figures well over quota and very little price cutting to keep the volume up. An excellent performer. Of course, the nature of the sales territories must also be considered before placing all credit or all blame on the sales representative.

## Customer Reports

Customer reports include a sales quota for each major customer and the variance reported on a monthly basis and year to date.

The manager is able to use these reports to identify any particular problems with customers. The average number of collection days for each customer usually appears on the same report.

## Control of Travel and Entertainment Costs

Control of travel and entertainment costs is more complex and even more important than it used to be. Most entertainment expenses are no longer tax-deductible, and fringe benefits tax also affects the situation. Travel and entertainment expenses are linked to the number of calls made rather than to the value of sales produced. Although accountants may feel that travel and entertainment should produce sales revenue it would not be logical to make spending on them dependent on sales being made. A decrease in sales revenue would mean less could be spent on travel and entertainment expenses. However, it would not make sense to decrease sales effort when sales are down. It would make more sense to increase the sales effort. This, of course, brings us to control of the types of claims made as expenses, and there are a thousand stories told of man's ingenuity in cheating on the 'swindle sheets'.

There is one about the new salesman who had just returned from his first tour of the rural areas. He handed his expenses sheet to the sales manager.

'Now, let's see. Motels, that looks okay. Petrol fair enough. Entertainment, a bit high but it'll do. Postage, stationery. What's this? One pair of imported Italian shoes, $120. You're joking! We don't pay for that sort of thing. Are you trying me on?'

'No. I wore out a pair of shoes making all the calls you had down, and I thought it was fair enough that I get a new pair.'

'Well that's what you think. You buy your own Italian shoes. Never try that stunt again.' The sales manager crossed off the claim for the shoes, reduced the total signed the sheet and gave it back.

'Now. Give that to the accountant.'

A month later, after another country tour the salesman was back. The sales manager went through the expense sheet, item by item.

'Motels, okay. Petrol bit heavy but not too bad. Entertainment, that's all right. Postage, stationery, that's okay. I'm glad to see that you've learnt your lesson. No expensive imported Italian shoes on here this time.' He signed the sheet and handed it to the salesman.

'Thanks', said the salesman. 'They're there all right. It's just that you can't find them.'

Control of revenue centres is complex and it is difficult to make generalisations because the problems differ so much from situation to situation. In some companies, efforts have been made to set standards for marketing expenses then to extract specific variances, but this is costly of time and resources and appears to provide little useful additional information. Once again it is a matter of cost/benefit.

# 13

# Profit Centres and Investment Centres

No, Murgatroyd. Just because Moses was given the Ten Commandments on Mt Sinai that doesn't make it a profit centre.

**Profit Centres**

A profit centre is a business segment which is responsible for making a planned level of profit. Many company groups or conglomerates operate as a group of profit centres. In some cases companies treat each branch as a profit centre, but this is quite unusual. An investment centre is responsible for achieving a pre-determined rate of return on the assets used.

Usually one major objective of a business organisation is to produce profits. In a profit centre we have a sub-unit which is required to aim for the same goals as the firm as a whole. If each of the sub-units reaches its goal so will the whole company. Profit centres come into existence when a sub-unit already markets products independent of other parts of the organisation. Top management will therefore, require the matching of revenue and expenses to achieve a reasonable profit contribution to the business as a whole. The manager of the profit centre must have sufficient control of the elements of the profit equation, that is, revenue and expense, to be able to make decisions which affect the elements and the subsequent profit.

Profit centres usually require managers with an entrepreneurial attitude. As a general rule the manager of a profit centre requires a broader level of education and experience than managers of cost centres or revenue centres.

## Setting Objectives for Profit Centres

Setting the objective for a profit centre is, to a certain extent, similar to what is required in a small business. In chapter 5 we saw how a firm may go about setting a target profit. However, a profit centre has no separate equity capital on which to set a cost of equity capital so the basis used to set the target profit figure is different. The usual basis is some return on assets percentage. In its simplest form, this is:

$$\frac{\text{Profit}}{\text{Assets used}} \text{ expressed as a percentage return rate}$$

There are some difficulties in this, the first being to decide on a required rate of return. This may be set according to past performance but may be adjusted for current economic conditions. The performance of competitors and other divisions of the same company may also be taken into consideration. The decision may be quite arbitrary although the rate required must clearly be in excess of financing costs.

The valuation basis for assets used is often a contentious issue. Sometimes the book value (cost less accumulated depreciation) is used. This may mean that the basis used has nothing to do with the current value of the assets and the rate of return means very little. Some firms use historical cost of the assets (ignoring depreciation) as a basis for the calculation. Others use current cost of similar assets or replacement cost. It does not matter much which one is used as long as there is consistency. Another problem is that profit means different things to different people. Some firms use gross margin, some use net profit of the division. Again, as long as everybody understands what base is used and there is consistency, it does not matter.

When all of this becomes too difficult, because a basis of asset value is too difficult or controversial a firm may decide instead to use a target return on sales. The rate of return selected will be based on past performance. In general terms, this will be the simple calculation:

$$\frac{\text{Profit}}{\text{Sales}} \text{ expressed as a percentage return rate}$$

The actual target profit figure would become the target rate of return on sales, multiplied by budgeted sales.

Once the target profit is established, the budget must set out the means of achieving it. After consideration of strategies to be adopted, divisional management may produce a budgeted profit and loss statement similar to that shown in chapter 7. Usually, the figures for previous periods are included side by side for comparison purposes. Top management will consider the budgeted profit and loss statement, particularly any variations of emphasis or effect compared with previous periods.

They may require adjustments to be made. When top management is convinced that the budgeted statement is feasible and acceptable, it will be approved, together with the provision of resources required. There may be a great deal of negotiation, argument and to-ing and fro-ing before formal approval occurs. This process is best explained by use of an actual example.

**Figure 13.1**
**DAVIS COMPUTER SERVICES DIVISION**
Budgeted profit and loss, 1993

|  | Actual | | | Budget |
|---|---|---|---|---|
|  | 1990 | 1991 | 1992 | 1993 |
|  | $'000 | $'000 | $'000 | $'000 |
| *Sales* | | | | |
| Computer hardware | 120.2 | 210.4 | 280.6 | 360.0 |
| Computer software | 84.6 | 116.4 | 124.3 | 220.0 |
| Services | 10.8 | 20.6 | 30.4 | 48.0 |
|  | 215.6 | 347.4 | 435.3 | 628.0 |
| *Cost of sales* | | | | |
| Computer hardware | 60.3 | 120.8 | 150.3 | 164.8 |
| Computer software | 48.4 | 59.6 | 61.1 | 112.8 |
| Services | 4.6 | 9.4 | 14.2 | 28.0 |
| *Marketing expenses* | | | | |
| Advertising | 10.0 | 10.1 | 10.5 | 15.6 |
| Salaries and commission | 28.2 | 29.4 | 30.6 | 31.2 |
| Research | 1.1 | 2.4 | 3.1 | 4.0 |
| *Administration expenses* | | | | |
| Salaries | 11.4 | 12.8 | 14.2 | 28.6 |
| Staff training | 4.0 | 6.2 | 7.1 | 10.2 |
| Materials | 1.3 | 1.2 | 1.3 | 1.4 |
| Facilities | 1.1 | 1.1 | 1.0 | 1.3 |
| *Finance expenses* | | | | |
| Interest | 6.2 | 6.1 | 6.3 | 12.4 |
| TOTAL EXPENSES | 176.6 | 259.1 | 299.7 | 410.3 |
| DIVISION CONTRIBUTION TO NET PROFIT | 39.0 | 88.3 | 135.6 | 217.7 |

Figure 13.1 shows a budgeted profit and loss statement for Davis Computer Services Division. There are a few points about this budget which may lead to its being queried by top management:

1 Is the near-doubling of revenue from software sales feasible? The division may reply that it is feasible because of a new market that they have just penetrated or a special sales effort being made this year.

2. Is the nearly 60 per cent increase in services feasible? The division may argue that new resources are being put into this part of the business as surveys indicate great growth potential.

3. Why is there a sudden drop in the ratio of cost of sales to sales revenue in computer hardware. In all previous years, cost of sales has been around 60 per cent of the sales revenue. Next year's projection is for it to be under 50 per cent. The division may reply that a new deal has been signed with a supplier to supply a new brand with larger retail margins.

4. Why is services cost of sales going to double? The answer to this one is simple. An additional person is to be taken on in this area to build up the activity to new levels.

5. Why are administration salaries to double? Again, the answer to this one is in additional hours being required to cope with the expanded business.

6. Why the extra allowance for staff training? With new employees starting they will require orientation into the company and existing employees will be required to take on new tasks also.

7. Why the increase in interest bill? It has doubled. Well top management should know the answer to that. They set the rates charged to divisions on the resources used.

So the bargaining process will continue until all of these matters are resolved and the budget is adopted. Then, as in any business situation, the emphasis will change from planning to control as the budget becomes the guide against which actual performance is compared.

There are some common problems involved in profit centre reporting. Time and time again the managers I talk to say that the biggest problem of all is transfer pricing.

## Transfer Pricing Between Divisions

One manager in a seminar I conducted said:

"The parent company is completely unreasonable. I manage a minerals division. We produce a mineral that the parent company requires in its processing. We could sell it anywhere in the world for $200 a tonne. They take it off us for $120. 1 wouldn't mind so much except they keep sending their stupid efficiency experts to tell me that we're not doing well enough. One little twerp just out of University told me that they were thinking of closing us up because we weren't making enough profit."

Sound familiar? It happens all over the place, every day. But it shouldn't.

Where segments of a company do business with each other, there is frequently a problem with the price that should be put on goods and services transferred from one segment to another. A good example of this is provided by the mining industry.

The Mining Division mines raw materials that are then transferred to the Refining Division. Once the mineral is refined, it is transferred to the Manufacturing Division for processing into the finished product. Two transfers of goods have taken place within the company between profit centres. At what price should these goods be transferred? It is important because each division is required to produce its target profit regardless of the company's overall result. If the transfer price is too low, the division buying will have its profit inflated and the division selling will be penalised. If the transfer price is too high, the selling division will make an unfair profit and the buying division will be penalised. The problem is complicated by the fact that often each division may also be selling to outsiders and may have access to supplies from outsiders. No wonder there are so many disputes about transfer price.

The most common bases used in setting a transfer price are cost (either full cost or variable cost only), market price and negotiated market price. Many firms make transfers between divisions based on cost, without making any allowance for a profit margin. This cost basis may be either variable costs only, where only the variable costs are included in the transfer price; or full cost, where both variable and fixed costs are included in the transfer price.

The major defect of this approach is that the only division that will show a profit is the one that makes the final sale to the outside world. This makes it difficult to measure performance in the other divisions in any meaningful way. Another defect is that this method allows one division to pass any inefficiencies in its cost structure on to another division, and there is no incentive for the selling division to control its costs. The final selling division is burdened with all of the inefficiencies, waste and cost padding of all of the divisions involved in handling any part of its product. This is likely to adversely affect its rate of return.

Despite these weaknesses, the cost-based systems are commonly used because they are easily understood, readily calculated and justifiable on the basis of fact. If a cost basis is to be used, there is a good argument for it being, full cost, based on standard costs. This will avoid the problem of inefficiencies being passed on.

A further refinement of the cost basis is to use the basis of standard variable cost per unit plus lost contribution margin per unit on outside sales. This may be virtually the same as a standard selling price.

As a general rule, the experts regard market price as the best basis for transfer pricing. It is the approach most consistent with the philosophy of a profit centre. It makes performance evaluation based on profit feasible, because all divisions, not just the final seller, can calculate profits. The market price approach treats the divisions as if they were individual businesses with responsibility for their own profits. However, if a company decides to use the market price approach, it should have a set of rules such as the following.

1   The selling division must match all outside bona fide prices and will not be compelled to sell internally.

2   The buying division must purchase internally if the selling division's price is competitive.

3   An impartial board is established to arbitrate in cases of disagreements between divisions.

These rules are logical. If the selling division can sell outside for more than the buying division wishes to pay, it must be due to a cheaper alternative being available. The selling division should maximise its profits by selling at the best price it can get and the buying division should maximise its profits by buying at the lowest possible price. If both divisions maximise their profits, the overall profit must be maximised.

Problems arise in cases where there is no market price for the product either because it is not usable at that stage or because there are no other firms that use it. In these cases it is probably best to use the standard variable cost plus some negotiated percentage mark-up.

A market price may have to be negotiated for various reasons. Sometimes the true market price is difficult to ascertain or the volume of sales may warrant a substantial discount. Perhaps selling and administrative costs are lower on transfer sales or there is no market in the item at all. Maybe the selling division has idle capacity and can make the extra units at low marginal cost.

Often the basis settled upon will be the variable cost plus lost contribution margin. An example of this is Parrot Piping Ltd, which has a division that makes garden sprinkler systems and another division that supplies hose fittings. The sprinkler division has designed a new system which requires a brass junction component which the fittings division could make. There is difficulty over the transfer price and the two divisions have agreed to accept a price set on the variable cost plus contribution margin basis. The data available is:

Quantity demanded          10 000 fittings
Variable cost of production   $1.50 per fitting

If the component is made by the fittings division, that division will have to forgo production of other products with a total contribution margin of $24 000.

The lost contribution margin per unit of the new fitting is:

$$\frac{\$24\,000}{10\,000 \text{ fittings}} = \$2.40 \text{ per fitting}$$

The variable cost is $1.50 per fitting. So:

$$\text{Transfer price} = \$1.50 + 2.40$$
$$= \$3.90 \text{ per fitting}$$

Not all negotiated market prices work out as comfortably as this. There can be a lot of scratching, eye-gouging, kicking and screaming before the final agreement.

Despite the confusion in the general area of transfer pricing, three general rules can be stated.

- First, market price is a better basis than cost because it is fairer all round and allows the calculation of meaningful divisional profit figures.
- Second, if divisions have been given autonomy, their decisions should not be interfered with by top management even if what they are doing is not maximising overall profit. (The advantages of divisional autonomy will more than counter-balance any losses made.)
- Third, no matter what you do, someone will still be complaining.

## The Revenue Control Problem

Another major problem in managing profit centres is revenue control. The best way of looking at profit is to put it in the formula:

$$\left( \begin{array}{c} \text{Selling} \\ \text{price} \\ \text{per unit} \end{array} \times \begin{array}{c} \text{units} \\ \text{sold} \end{array} \right) - \left( \begin{array}{c} \text{Variable} \\ \text{costs} \\ \text{per unit} \end{array} \times \begin{array}{c} \text{units} \\ \text{sold} \end{array} \right) - \text{fixed costs}$$

All of the problems discussed with relation to cost centres and revenue centres still exist with profit centres. However, the manager of a profit centre can adjust the profit situation by either adjusting prices or adjusting costs, while the managers of cost centres and revenue centres have access to only one of those approaches.

If the management of a profit centre does not have full control over spending or pricing, then it is not logical to judge its effectiveness on the basis of profitability. Managers cannot validly be assessed according to measures over which they cannot exercise full control.

Anything which interferes with the divisional manager's control over costs damages the validity of measures of divisional performance. One example of such a situation is shared services. Many companies have certain centralised services such as finance, accounting, credit control planning, business economics and payroll. This may well be more efficient than decentralisation, but it causes problems of control and allocation to divisions. Even if some equitable basis for allocation can be found, such as a per person basis for payroll administration, the central division can pass its inefficiencies and waste on to the other divisions without penalty.

Another difficulty is sunk cost items. Many decisions made in the past continue to have effects. The decision to build a poorly designed plant may affect production for decades afterwards. It may not be economic to replace it and the current manager is committed to the expenses incurred. The poor design of the plant probably results in lack of flexibility in methods and production capacity.

Company-wide decisions also interfere with the divisional manager's control over costs. Advertising policy and capital expenditure decisions are likely examples. These kinds of decisions are centralised because they affect more than one division. A company has limited borrowing capacity, based on its profit and structure, so divisions can seldom be given the power to borrow without reference to top management.

Once the budget has set the expectations, then performance can be measured against the budget. The usual way of doing this is to set out the profit and loss statement with budgeted and actual figures, and the variances highlighted. Variances which reduce profit will be in brackets. So the brackets used do not necessarily mean that the actual figure is less than the budgeted figure; they mean that the actual figure is bad, that it reduces profit. The profit and loss statement with variances for Davis Computer Services Division is set out in Figure 13.2. (See Figure 13.1 for Davis's earlier report).

This comparison of budget with actual performance shows that top management was justified in its skepticism about the division's ability to almost double its sales of software. It did increase sales by fifty per cent but doubling sales in a year is very difficult. The comparison also shows that the new supplier of hardware has had the expected impact on margins; and performance has been almost dead on target. Services almost reached the expansion anticipated in the budget. The cost of software sales was down in line with the lower than expected levels of sales, and good control has been exercised over all costs. The final net profit contribution from the division is close to target, despite the lower-than-expected sales of software. In summary, considering the ambitious program of sales expansion that was built into the budget, the performance was very good.

**Figure 13.2**
**DAVIS COMPUTER SERVICES DIVISION**
Budgeted and actual contribution to net profit, 1993

|  | Budgeted | Actual | Variance |
|---|---:|---:|---:|
|  | $'000 | $'000 | $'000 |
| *Sales* |  |  |  |
| Computer hardware | 360.0 | 362.4 | 2.4 |
| Computer software | 220.0 | 180.3 | (39.7) |
| Services | 48.0 | 46.4 | (1.6) |
|  | 628.0 | 589.1 | (38.9) |
| *Cost of sales* |  |  |  |
| Computer hardware | 164.8 | 166.4 | (1.6) |
| Computer software | 112.8 | 82.4 | 30.4 |
| Services | 28.0 | 29.3 | (1.3) |
| *Marketing expenses* |  |  |  |
| Advertising | 15.6 | 15.6 | — |
| Salaries and commission | 31.2 | 28.4 | 2.8 |
| Research | 4.0 | 4.0 | — |
| *Administration expenses* |  |  |  |
| Salaries | 28.6 | 29.8 | (1.2) |
| Staff training | 10.2 | 8.4 | 1.8 |
| Materials | 1.4 | 0.7 | 0.7 |
| Facilities | 1.3 | 0.8 | 0.5 |
| *Finance expenses* |  |  |  |
| Interest | 12.4 | 11.2 | 1.2 |
| **TOTAL EXPENSES** | 410.3 | 377.0 |  |
| **DIVISION CONTRIBUTION TO NET PROFIT** | 217.7 | 212.1 | (5.6) |

*Never ask of money spent*

*Where the spender thinks it went*

*Nobody was ever meant*

*To remember or invent*

*What he did with every cent*

--Robert Frost

## Investment Centres

The widest responsibilities and problems belong to managers of investment centres. As well as the work associated with cost centres, revenue centres and profit centres, they have a responsibility to increase profits as the investment in assets is increased. This increase must be at least in proportion to the amount of increased investment. Investment centre performance is usually measured either in terms of ROI (return on investment), or residual income.

To measure the performance of an investment centre, you must first value the amount invested. This creates two problems. Which assets do we include as part of the investment? And how do we value those assets?

Assets should be included if they are controllable by the manager, but it is likely that some assets not completely controllable by the manager will still be included. One of these is cash. Often cash is controlled by head office rather than within the division. If this is the case, a nominal amount may be included as a cash balance or it may be a notional amount based on turnover.

Another example is debtors. Again these are usually controlled centrally but they will be included at their actual amount as generated in that division. Since debtors may fluctuate, an average monthly figure may be used rather than the end-of-year balance sheet figure.

Inventories will be included at book value which should be 'the lower of cost or net realisable value'. A monthly average may be more appropriate than the balance sheet figure as stocks also fluctuate.

Fixed assets create difficulties because the book value in the balance sheet may have little relationship to market value or replacement value. If historical cost is used, there is the question of whether original cost or cost less accumulated depreciation (book value) should be used. Book value may be favoured but if it is used, it may make managers reluctant to replace old equipment as that will make the value of the asset base higher, and reduce the rate of return.

Assets being leased are another problem, as some leased assets do not appear in the balance sheet. These assets still contribute to the generation of profit so this will produce a false rate of return.

## Measuring Performance in an Investment Centre

The two most common methods used to measure success in investment centres are to:

- Calculate the return on assets. This is sometimes referred to as return on investment or ROI. However, since some other people use the term ROI for return on capital invested, this can be misleading.
- Residual income. This is a measure of the return obtained above a pre-set return on investment.

## Measuring Return on Investment (ROI)

A common way of measuring the success of an investment centre is to calculate its return on investment (ROI). In this case we will take this to be the same as return on assets used. Companies preset acceptable rates according to their cost of capital. Investment centres are required to achieve at least the required rate. Those which do not meet the required rate may be liquidated or slowly sold off. Investment centres with high rates of return may be expanded. The basis of the ROI calculation is the formula:

$$\frac{\text{Profit made by the division}}{\text{Value of the assets used}} \text{ expressed as a percentage}$$

Problems arise because of the possible different bases of asset valuation. For instance, consider the case of a division which has made a profit of $2 million; it has assets which cost $10 million, have been depreciated to $4 million, and would cost $20 million to replace.

$$\text{If ROI} = \frac{\text{Profit}}{\text{Original cost value of the assets}}$$

$$= \frac{\$2m}{\$10m}$$

$$= 20\%$$

$$\text{If ROI} = \frac{\text{Profit}}{\text{Book value of the assets}}$$

$$= \frac{\$2m}{\$4m}$$

$$= 50\%$$

$$\text{If ROI} = \frac{\text{Profit}}{\text{Replacement cost of the assets}}$$

$$= \frac{\$2m}{\$20m}$$

$$= 10\%$$

Which is correct? The answer is all of them. Different companies use different bases and all have their advantages and disadvantages. This uncertainty leads to the use of an alternative method of measuring the performance of an investment centre. It is referred to as the residual income method.

## Residual Income

Residual income (Rl) is the profit that an investment centre is able to earn above a minimum rate of return on operating assets. We shall compare this with the ROI method using the data from our last example:

|  | ROI | RI |
|---|---|---|
| Average operating assets | (a) $4 million | $4 million |
| Profit of division | (b) $2 million | $2 million |
| ROI (b ÷ a) | 50% |  |
| Less: Minimum rate of return required (assumed to be 15% on the assets of $4 million) |  | 600 000 |
| RESIDUAL INCOME |  | $1 400 000 |

Under the residual income method, the performance of the division is judged according to how large or small the residual income figure may be. The bigger the better. Bonuses are often calculated as a set proportion of residual income.

It is sometimes argued that the residual income method encourages managers to make investments that may have been rejected by a manager working under the ROI basis. To take an example, consider the situation where a manager is faced with the opportunity of investing in new plant costing $1 million which will earn $200,000 a year in extra profit. The effect will be as follows:

|  | ROI | RI |
|---|---|---|
| Average operating assets | $5 million | $5 million |
| Profit of division | $2 200 000 | $2 200 000 |
| ROI | 44% | |
| Less: Minimum rate of return required (15%) | | 750 000 |
| RESIDUAL INCOME | | $1 450 000 |

Under the ROI method, the manager may reject the investment because it reduces the division's ROI but under the residual income method it would be accepted because it increases the residual income.

The major disadvantage of the residual income method is in situations where divisions are of different sizes. Consider the situation of Division Y and Division Z at Hatcher Industries Ltd:

|  | Division Y | Division Z |
|---|---|---|
| Average operating assets | $2 million | $400 000 |
| Profit of division | $300 000 | $100 000 |
| ROI | 15% | 25% |
| Minimum rate of return required (12%) | $240 000 | 48 000 |
| RESIDUAL INCOME | $ 60 000 | $ 52 000 |

The residual income method indicates a better performance by the manager of Division Y, but the rate of return on assets used is much better in the smaller division (Z). To use this as a basis of comparison where the size of divisions is so different, puts the management of the smaller division at a severe disadvantage.

In practice, the ROI method is used much more frequently than the residual income method to judge performance of investment centres. Whichever method is used, management performance is the key to job survival.

Two divisional managers were having lunch together and one was telling the other:

'Over at our place we've got this terrific competition going between the divisional managers. The one with the best ROI result gets a trip for two to Europe. The second highest gets a car, and the third highest gets a $1000 clothing voucher. You should see the way the place is buzzing.'

The other manager stared vacantly into the coffee cup then looked up.

'We're having much the same sort of thing over at our place too. The manager that wins gets to keep a job.'

# 14

## Taxes and More Taxes

'The art of taxation consists in so plucking the goose as to obtain the largest amount of feathers with the least possible amount of hissing.'

--J. B. Colbert, 1680
(Superintendent of finance to
King Louis XIV of France)

'Death and taxes are inevitable.'

--T. C. Haliburton, 1854
(Canadian humorist, judge and
politician)

'The Australian tax system . . . has become confiscatory in its impact, savagely unfair in its distribution, and a menace to our survival as a healthy and buoyant community.'

--Peter Clyne, 1979

'Help!'

--Eric Smith, 1991

In recent years there has been something of a revolution in the way in which we are taxed. The methods used, and the emphasis on various types of taxation have changed. However, taxes abound at every level of government: federal state and local. This chapter can only serve as a broad outline of the types of taxes that may affect the business executive. There are plenty of specialty books available to help you if you need details about a particular tax, including some excellent free booklets available from the Taxation Office.

## PAYE Income Tax

The tax that is most heavily felt by us as individuals is personal income tax, but it does not have great relevance to business managers. We will look at the tax briefly then concentrate on those areas that concern business. Personal income tax is a progressive tax, that is, the higher the level of income, the higher the 'per dollar' rate of tax. The taxation rates applied at 30 June, 1991 were:

| Taxable Income per annum $ | Marginal rate per $ (in cents) |
| --- | --- |
| 0 - 5,250 | 0 |
| 5,250 - 17,649 | 20.5 |
| 17,650 - 20,599 | 24.5 |
| 20,600 - 20,699 | 29.5 |
| 20,700 - 34,999 | 38.5 |
| 35,000 - 35,999 | 42.5 |
| 36,000 - 49,999 | 46.5 |
| 50,000 and above | 47.0 |

In all cases add 1.25% for Medicare levy.

This means that although the top part of your income above $35,000 may be taxed at 49 cents in the dollar, the remainder of your income is still taxed at the lower rates. Therefore, the average rate of tax is substantially lower than your marginal rate. As an example, on the rates above, a person with a taxable income of $40,000 will pay total tax of $11,085 which is an average rate of 28 per cent. Much too high, but not as bad as you might expect.

Of course, the Medicare levy is in addition to this tax. The Medicare levy is 1.25 per cent of your taxable income with no upper limit. It is not payable on incomes below $11,746.

One of the major responsibilities of the employer is to deduct tax from employees' wages and salaries. This Pay-as-you-earn (PAYE) tax system aims at collecting tax from wage and salary earners in the year in which it is earned. The Taxation Office supplies schedules of the deductions that should be made. A taxpayer may make a Tax Installment Declaration on the appropriate form in order to claim exemption from PAYE deductions for the tax-free part of earnings (the first $5 250). If the claim is not made, the adjustment is made in the calculation of tax payable at the end of the year, anyway. When the employer deducts the tax from employees' earnings, the taxation money must be forwarded to the Taxation Office by the seventh day of the following month. Employers who have large numbers of employees are required to do this twice each month, on the 7th and 21st days of the month. Employers who fail to comply with this requirement are severely treated because they are effectively using the money as an interest-free loan.

Any employer who employs five or more employees must register as a group employer within seven days after becoming that employer. An employer of less than five employees can request to become a group employer. The other option for the employer of less than five people is to use the tax stamps method of attaching tax stamps to a sheet. It makes no difference whether the employer is a company or an individual.

As well as sending in the tax money deducted, the group employer must prepare a group certificate for each employee in quadruplicate on the prescribed form and give the employee the original and triplicate of the group certificate by 14 July in each year. An employee who leaves during the year must be given a group certificate within seven days of leaving. This particular provision is often ignored by employers and very few seem to be prosecuted.

The employer must also send the duplicate of the group certificate to the Taxation Office between 30 June and 14 August, together with a reconciliation statement reconciling the tax money sent to the Taxation Office with the total installment deductions on the group certificates. The employer must not make alterations on the group certificate or prepare any more after sending the reconciliation to the Taxation Office.

An employer who is not a group employer is required to keep a tax deduction sheet for each employee showing salary or wages paid and the deductions made. Every four weeks the employer must purchase tax stamps from the post office and affix them to the tax deduction sheet. The tax stamps must equal the amount of deductions and must be canceled in ink.

In the case of either method of tax collection, the employer who fails to make deductions as required is liable to a fine of $1000 for each failure to do so. In addition the employer must pay the amount that should have been deducted. It is not a defence that the employee asked for deductions not to be made. The responsibility is with the employer.

## Provisional Income Tax

If a person receives income which is not subject to tax installments being deducted by an employer, such as dividends, interest, rents, business income and royalties, and that income is $1000 or more in a financial year, the person must pay provisional tax. Provisional tax effectively means that you must pay tax on the next year's income in advance. In the 1990/91 tax year, for example, you would have to pay provisional tax on your total non-PAYE taxed earnings for 1989/90 plus 11 per cent for inflation and potential earnings growth.

If the amount of provisional tax is below $8 000 this tax would be payable by 31 March 1991. There is a further provision that where a person's previous year's provisional tax was over $8 000, the person must make quarterly installments on 1 September, 1 December, 1 March and 1 June.

If you have reason to believe that earnings subject to provisional tax will be less in the following year, you can make a voluntary self-assessment and have the tax varied. But you had better be right because penalty rates apply if you underestimate the tax payable by more than 10 per cent.

Tax paid as provisional tax is credited by the Taxation Office to your account. When you make your taxation return, the actual tax payable is calculated and matched against your payments. A refund is made (without interest) if you have paid too much.

In a new business, provisional tax often comes as a rude shock. In the first year of operation the owner will probably pay no tax. Then after 30 June a tax form will be sent to the Taxation Office. The Taxation Office will calculate tax payable and send a demand for that amount plus provisional tax for the next year. So two years' tax must be paid from the one year's income. In any small business, it pays to put aside part of the profits in a special taxation account to allow for this. As Peter Clyne says in Outlaw Among Lawyers:

'You have to pay that extra $5000 so that the fiscal fiend doesn't have to chase you for it in the following year. He is the only creditor on earth who can collect money before it is due to him.'

## Prescribed Payments Scheme

You've probably seen delivery vans around with stickers on them protesting against the prescribed payments scheme. They usually read 'Private Business not Employees' or something similar. The scheme was part of the government initiative against the so-called 'cash economy'. Many people who receive cash payments during the year may be able to leave large parts of their income out when declaring it for taxation purposes. The prescribed payments scheme attempts to overcome this by treating private contractors in the industries where the worst abuses occurred in much the same way as PAYE income earners.

Amounts called 'prescribed payments deductions' must be deducted from payments made to them by the people they do business with and forwarded to the Taxation Office. It is a separate scheme from PAYE. Any payment that is made under a contract which mainly involves the performance of work may be a prescribed payment if it falls in the industry groups specifically mentioned in the Act.

Generally speaking the payments are those made by contractors to sub-contractors but there are exceptions in the building and construction and transport industries where payments between contractors may be included in the scheme. In the building industry when a project costs more than $10 000, even householders contracting with a builder will have to make deductions and forward them to the Taxation Office.

The scheme only covers certain industries. These are the motor-vehicle repair industry, joinery and cabinet-making services, architectural services, engineering services, surveying services, professional building and construction services of any kind, the cleaning industry, the building and construction industry, and the road transport industry. In the road transport industry the prescribed payments scheme only applies to situations where the user of the service engages the vehicle on a regular daily basis in 'tied ownership', 'captive fleet' and similar arrangements.

Persons or businesses who are liable to make a prescribed payment must register with the Taxation Office. Prescribed payments are recorded on a deduction form which is completed monthly by both the payer and payee. Tax is deducted by the payer at 15 per cent of the gross payment; if the payee has not provided the payer with a deduction form or has not filled it out properly, the payer must make deductions at 30 per cent of the gross payment.

The originals of the deduction form completed by both payer and payee, the tax deducted and a reconciliation form must be sent to the Taxation Office by the payer by the fourteenth day of the following month, and the payee is credited with the tax paid. At the end of the year, the payee lodges duplicates of all the deduction forms. When the tax is assessed, the deductions made are used to reduce the tax payer's liability. It is likely, however, that the deductions made will not fully cover the tax payer's liability and further payments may be required. The prescribed payments scheme does not exempt the payees involved from having to pay provisional tax.

## Company Income Tax

Companies are treated as separate tax paying entities which pay company income tax. The main difference in the treatment of companies is that there is a flat rate of tax on company profits rather than a progressive rate. At the moment the rate is 39 cents in the dollar. So even if a company made only $10 profit for the year, it must pay $3.90 in tax. Companies, like individuals, can deduct all of the expenses of earning revenue from that revenue in calculating assessable income.

Until recently, company profits were taxed twice, first with company income tax and then as dividend income of the shareholders. This could mean that if a company made a $100,000 profit, the Taxation Office would receive most of it, particularly as some shareholders were on a 60 cents in the dollar personal income tax rate.

| PROFIT | $100 000 |
|---|---|
| Less: Company tax at old rate of 46¢ per $ | 46 000 |
| Distributed to shareholders | 54 000 |
| Assume shareholders on old top tax rate 60¢ per $ | 32 400 |
| NET LEFT FOR SHAREHOLDERS | $21 600 |

The Taxation Office had the other $78,600.

Since 1988, the company income tax rate has been 39 cents per dollar and dividend imputation has been introduced.

## The Dividend Imputation System

Under dividend imputation as introduced from 1 July 1987, dividends received by taxpayers are free of income tax provided the company has paid tax at the normal 39 in the $ rate. Dividends paid out of profits where the normal company tax rate has not been paid will not be exempt from tax. This means that in the case of the $100,000 profit made now by a company:

| | |
|---|---|
| PROFIT | $100 000 |
| Less: Company tax at new rate of 39¢ per $ | $39 000 |
| Distributed to shareholders | $61 000 |

No further tax is payable.

Even better, a shareholder who is below the 39 per $ rate of personal tax, that is, a person with a taxable income of less than $35,000, can claim rebates against other income to reduce overall tax liability.

Since dividends are virtually tax-free and capital gains on shares are now taxable, shareholders may now exert pressure for bigger dividends than in the past. This may have severe implications for funding of companies. However, since bonus shares are to be treated as dividends for purposes of imputation, it is likely that companies will issue many more bonus shares rather than pay larger cash dividends. However, bonus shares are usually taxable under the capital gains tax.

Superannuation funds are exempt from tax anyway, so dividend imputation has no benefits for them. It is likely that they might gradually move out of share investment into property and the financial markets where their tax-free status will give them an advantage.

## Entertainment Expenses are not Usually Tax Deductible

Before 19 September, 1985 entertainment expenses which were related to business were tax-deductible, provided they were incurred in producing income. Except in very limited circumstances, these expenses are no longer deductible. This does not mean that the business is not allowed to take clients to dinner, it simply means that it is no longer tax-deductible. It is claimed that this has had a catastrophic effect on the restaurant industry. The only entertainment expenses deductible for the firm are the following:

- Normal everyday meals for staff in the staff canteen.
- Everyday meals for directors in the executive dining room.
- Meals for an employee while traveling on business or any other person acting on behalf of the firm, but not a meal consumed while entertaining another person.
- Meals connected with attendance at a seminar related to business.
- Meals provided to employees under an industrial award.
- Running costs of food and drink vending machines provided primarily for employees.
- Meals for restaurant or hotel staff where the employer is in that industry.
- Recreational facilities, swimming pools and sports facilities provided for employees on workdays.
- Entertainment allowances paid to employees or directors.
- Gifts and entertainment to purchasers or the general public as a means of promotion.

All other entertainment expenses are non-deductible. A myth seems to have grown up that provided the client is entertained on the firm's premises, no matter how lavishly, this will be tax deductible. This is, in fact, only true if the client is attending an approved seminar, but there is some vagueness in the definition of 'seminar'.

In the case of the individual employee or director, tax deductible entertainment expenses are restricted to these:

- The cost of your own meals while traveling on business, unless this is in the course of entertaining another person. (Eat alone.)
- The cost of meals in overtime where there is an overtime meal allowance in your award.
- The cost of meals, travel and accommodation which is reasonably associated with attending a business-related seminar.
- Normal entertainment where the employer is in the entertainment industry.

You will notice that nowhere at any time are entertainment expenses tax-deductible if fellow employees, customers or suppliers are being entertained.

Travel expenses to and from work are not an allowable tax deduction. However, the following are tax-deductible items.

- Any travel expenses incurred in doing your job, less any reimbursement from the employer. Travel expenses between two distinct jobs in two separate locations provided you pay tax on the income from both. (If you have a business at home and a salaried job elsewhere, part of the travel costs from home to salaried job may be allowable if it is necessary to earning the income in the home business.)
- Any travel costs incurred as a condition of your employment.

Claims for travel expenses are subject to strict Taxation Office rules. If you are involved, you should obtain the details from the Taxation Office.

## Capital Gains Tax

The capital gains tax is a part of the income tax legislation. It was introduced to block tax avoidance schemes which converted taxable income into non-taxable capital gains. The tax is charged on real gains (adjusted for inflation) which have been realised through sale of an asset acquired by the taxpayer after 19 September 1985.

Capital gains are taxed at the same marginal rates as any other income. Realised capital losses can be offset against any capital gains in the same year or a later year.

The way in which the taxable gain is calculated depends on whether the asset is a non-personal use asset, such as shares or property; a listed personal-use asset on the specific list provided in the act, such as a work of art or an antique; or a non-listed personal-use asset, such as a car or piece of furniture.

The following assets are specifically excluded from capital gains tax:

- Assets acquired before 20 September 1985.
- The tax payer's principal place of residence (that is, your house; other residences such as holiday homes are not exempt). Most compensation and damages received.
- Winnings from lotteries, betting, gambling or a game of prizes.
- One-fifth of the goodwill where a business is sold for less than one million dollars.
- Cash gifts in Australian currency.
- Most superannuation benefits (but these may be taxed under other provisions).
- Inheritances from deceased estates.
- Non-listed personal-use assets sold for less than $5000 each. The copyrights of an Australian film.

- Trading stock.
- Assets sold within twelve months if profits are already taxable, such as capital gains on shares.
- Decorations awarded for valor or brave conduct where they were not purchased by the seller.
- Most motor cars including vintage and veteran cars.
- Certain rights of insurers under insurance policies.

There are strict provisions to prevent acquisitions of assets being back-dated to before 20 September 1985.

The amount of capital gain is the difference between the cost of the asset plus improvements made, and the selling price, adjusted for inflation. The rate of inflation is taken to be that indicated by the Consumer Price Index. All of this is best explained by means of an example.

On 1 October 1985 Ann Martin purchased a country retreat, a little run-down cottage in which to regain her sanity at weekends. Because it was not her principal place of residence, it was subject to capital gains tax when sold. The purchase price was $40 000; acquisition costs (legal fees, stamp duty, etc.) were $2500. Improvements were commenced in July 1986 which cost $11 000. The cottage was sold on 1 July 1988 for $88 000, and disposal costs (advertising, commission, etc.) were $3500. The consumer price index over this period was 100 on 1 October 1985, 110 on 1 July 1986, and 125 on 1 July 1988. The capital gain made on the cottage is calculated as follows.

|  |  |  |  |
|---|---|---|---|
| Amount received from sale | | | $88 000 |
| Less: Indexed cost of property: | | | |
| Property | $40 000 | | |
| Acquisition costs | 2 500 | | |
| $\dfrac{\text{CPI 1988 } 125}{\text{CPI 1985 } 100} \times$ | 42 500 | $53 125 | |
| Capital improvements: | | | |
| $\dfrac{125}{100} \times \$11\,000$ | | 12 500 | |
| Cost of disposal | | 3 500 | 69 125 |
| TAXABLE CAPITAL GAIN | | | $18 875 |

If Ann is on the maximum marginal tax rate of 47 cents in the dollar, she would be required to pay capital gains tax of $8 871, leaving a real gain of $10 004 after tax. In summary, here are a few points to note about capital gains tax:

1. It does not apply to your principal residence so you can make any amount of capital gain on your home and not have to pay tax on it. This has led to a boom in house improvements.

2. The tax is not payable on assets acquired before 20 September 1985 regardless of when they are sold and how much capital gain is made.

3. The tax is not payable until the asset is disposed of. It is not assessed on estimated gains in value.

4. It is payable by companies as well as individuals.

5. Bonus shares issued to shareholders are subject to capital gains tax if the shares on which the bonus is given were acquired after 19 September, 1985. The acquisition date of a bonus share is deemed to be the date when the original share was acquired. So bonus shares on shares purchased before 20 September 1985 by the tax payer are not assessable for capital gains tax.

Capital gains tax may also apply to personal-use assets. A personal-use asset is one which is owned primarily for its personal use or enjoyment. Personal-use assets are classified into two categories, listed and non-listed. Listed personal-use assets are treated in much the same way as non-listed personal-use assets, like property. However, any losses made on disposal can only be offset against gains made on other listed personal-use assets in that or later periods. Listed personal-use assets are those included on a special list. The list applies to any asset which costs over $100 and which is:

- a print, etching, drawing, painting, sculpture or similar work of art
- jewelry
- a rare folio, rare manuscript or rare book
- a postage stamp or first-day cover
- a coin or medallion
- an antique
- an interest in such an asset or
- a debt owed or an option or right to acquire such an asset.

The calculation of taxable capital gains for any of these listed assets is the same as that for non-listed personal-use assets. Non-listed personal-use assets do not attract capital gains tax unless they are sold for more than $5 000 each.

## Fringe Benefits Tax (FBT)

Fringe benefits tax (FBT) is payable by employers, not employees. It is in the nature of a federal payroll tax on fringe benefits provided to employees. The benefits on which the tax is payable include:

- cars provided for private use
- interest-free or low-interest loans
- private expenses of employees paid by the employer, such as school fees and health insurance

- cancellation of debts owed by employees
- provision of residential accommodation
- living-away-from-home allowances
- discounted air travel
- free or discounted goods or property
- entertainment provided
- rights to the use of property

The intention of the provisions are to reduce the use of fringe benefits as non-taxable employee rewards. Previously, if an employee took a pay rise, the additional income was taxable, but if the company gave the use of a car or paid school fees this was not taxable. (Officially it was taxable but the section was too uncertain to be properly enforced.) The legislation places the obligation on the business to keep all records and make a self-assessment for the tax. The FBT return must be made by 28 April in each year.

Payments are by quarterly installments due on 28 July, 28 October, 28 January and with the return on 28 April. Installments are to be paid in advance on the basis of one-quarter of the previous year's liability for FBT. No installments are payable if less than $1000 was paid in the previous year. There are penalties for failure to make a return, making false statements or avoiding the tax. The FBT tax rate is 49 cents in the dollar.

There are detailed rules about the way in which benefits are to be valued. Employers should remember that the FBT provisions are designed specifically to make it costly and difficult to provide fringe benefits, so that they will give easily-taxed pay rises instead. The Taxation Office provides detailed information about how the benefits are valued and what records must be kept.

## Sales Tax

Sales tax is a major federal tax which is applied at the wholesale level on the wholesale value of all new taxable goods used in Australia. Second-hand goods are treated as new goods if they are imported. The tax is usually levied at the point where the goods are sold from wholesaler to retailer. All companies and individuals who carry on business in Australia as wholesalers or manufacturers must register as sales tax payers. There are exemptions where average annual sales are below $12 000 or tax payable would be less than $250.

Sales tax payers are given a sales tax number. If this number is quoted in a purchase from another manufacturer or wholesaler, sales tax will not be payable on that transaction.

The rate of sales tax payable, which is of course incorporated into the price passed on to the consumer, is generally 20 per cent on the wholesale sale value. However, six schedules govern the situation. The First Schedule exempts certain goods from sales tax. The exemption may be unconditional or conditional upon the purchaser. An unconditional exemption applies to most foods, medicines, pharmaceuticals, fuels, building materials, clothing and footwear. An exemption which is conditional upon the purchaser applies to goods purchased by some organisations. Examples are goods used by government departments, charities or schools.

The Second Schedule (30 per cent tax rate) places a 30 per cent sales tax on luxury goods such as furs, cosmetics, cameras, jewelry, television sets, radios, VCRs and stereos.

The Third Schedule (10 per cent tax rate) has two categories: unconditional which includes all household goods, hand tools and packaging equipment; or conditional depending on the specific use of the equipment. (For instance, equipment used repairing motor vehicles is in the conditional category.)

The Fourth Schedule (20 per cent tax rate) covers all commercial motor vehicles, but excludes passenger cars, motor cycles, tractors and spare parts. Passenger cars are covered by the Fifth Schedule (also 20 per cent tax rate).

The Sixth Schedule (10 per cent tax rate) impinges on the food area to a certain extent as it covers wine, cider, mead and other fermented alcoholic drinks. It also includes flavoured milk, snack foods and some aerated waters.

Sales tax payers must register within twenty-eight days of starting business or risk a fine of $250 per day for failure to do so. Invoices must show sales tax charged as a separate figure. Monthly returns must be filed showing details of sales tax transactions, by the twenty-first day of the next month.

## Payroll Tax

The state government starts to get into the act with payroll tax. This is levied on salaries and wages paid to employees including commissions, bonuses, directors' fees and the cost of providing meals and accommodation. Some organisations, like churches, charities, schools, public hospitals, local councils and trade unions, are exempt. Legislation varies from state to state as to the amount of the tax and rebates for decentralisation and youth employment. Small employers are exempted in all states.

## Stamp Duty

Stamp duty is also a state tax. The provisions of stamp duty legislation vary greatly from state to state, but nearly all financial instruments and large transactions will bear some stamp duty as it is the states' largest source of taxation revenue. For example, if you purchase a house for $200 000, you will pay over $10 000 in stamp duty. Full details are available from state taxation offices.

## Excise Duty

Excise is a duty charge similar to customs duty, rather than a tax, since it is charged not on value but on volume - so much per liter of spirits, per kilo of tobacco, per liter of petrol. It is a federal government duty which makes up a substantial part of the price of those products where it is applied.

## Local Government Taxes

Rates on property are usually based on the value of the land occupied; however, some councils rate the property according to net annual value, which is a rating based on property improvements.

The wide-ranging taxes mentioned in this chapter are not the full range possible, they are only a sampling of what there is and what may affect you either directly or indirectly. As a general rule, far more is gained from arranging matters to minimise their impact rather than attempting to evade them or fight them.

Politicians have always seen the collection of taxes as a right rather than a privilege.

There is a true story about William Gladstone, Britain's great Prime Minister of the late nineteenth century. One day while he was Chancellor of the Exchequer, in charge of the Treasury, he attended a lecture given by the brilliant physicist Michael Faraday. Faraday was demonstrating some of the potential wonders of electricity. When the lecture was over, Gladstone shook Faraday's hand and said:

'What you spoke about, Mr Faraday, is purely theoretical. But tell me does it have any practical value?'

'What do you mean by "practical value"?' Faraday asked.

'I mean,' replied Gladstone, 'can it be taxed?'

At this stage you may want to be philosophical. It's a strange world we live in. The strong take it away from the weak. The clever take it away from the strong. And the government takes it away from everybody.

# 15

## Service Industries

One of the most obvious changes in the business world is the growth in service industries. In all developed countries, service industries are the fastest growing sector. In Australia about 50 per cent of all businesses produce services rather than goods and it is estimated that by the year 2000 over 60 per cent of the Australian workforce will be employed in service industries.

The range of service industries extends from large international organisations like the major hotel chains through to one-person typing services operated from home. Some of the areas of business covered include hotels, restaurants, beauty parlors, manicure services, hairdressers, repair services, cinemas, theatres, nightclubs, television, radio, advertising, travel services, airlines, resorts, recreation and sporting services, sports clubs, legal services, accounting, marketing, education, architecture, banking, finance companies, financial advisors, computer services, welfare organisations, churches, government services, plumbers, electricians, maintenance services, cleaning, artists, musicians, and so on and on. Some of the service businesses which used to be unglamorous are now regarded as regular goldmines. It's getting so that one of our major economic problems is what to do with the tremendous concentration of wealth in the hands of plumbers.

The major objective of a service business must be to provide a service for which there is an economic demand. Those who provide good service will prosper, those who provide poor service or over-priced service will fail.

I can remember once standing at a post office counter waiting for the assistant to notice me. I'm over 140 kilos and 183 centimeters tall, but she didn't seem to see me at all. She just went on pottering about on the side bench straightening things up and sorting out slips of paper while I and the other customers just stood there. Eventually I said in a loud voice:

'You can't complain about the service.'

'Why not?' the woman said, looking up at last.

'Because there isn't any.'

## The Special Characteristics of Service Industries

There are many special characteristics of service businesses so it is necessary to consider them as a separate category of businesses with their own problems.

1. **They have an intangible product.** This is the most obvious characteristic. In a service business the product is a service not a tangible product. With tangible products, the customer can see the product and judge its value and quality by inspecting it.

2. **Quality is usually judged on service.** In a service business quality is judged by the attitudes of those providing the service and the results of using the service. A very pleasant electrician who can't fix your kitchen lights is not much help to you. However, even if the job was successfully done, an unpleasant, rude and dirty electrician is unlikely to be recalled for further jobs.

    I was once treated like a criminal by a leading Sydney hotel because I wanted to pay cash for my room, not charge it. Needless to say I have never returned and have advised dozens of others not to go there either.

3. **There is usually little or no inventory.** Another characteristic is absence of inventory. A business which sells tangible goods can store them as inventory. The inventory can reduce the impact of fluctuations in sales. However, services cannot be stored. If the services available today are not used today, the revenue from those potential services is lost forever. A manufacturer can produce and store goods even if there is no current demand for the products. This will enable the firm to take advantage of larger production runs. Service businesses cannot do this. They must therefore be very efficient in time allocation if revenue is to be maximised. Available resources must be matched against customer demand as far as time is concerned.

4. **A service business generally has limited resources for sale**. Most service businesses have fixed resources, at least in the short run. A hotel cannot suddenly increase its number of rooms for rent because of a sudden surge in demand. If demand for rooms is down, some of the rooms or whole floors can be closed off but this does not substantially reduce costs because of the high ratio of fixed costs to variable costs. In a hospital it is very difficult to stand down some of the nursing staff in slack periods. So the matching of available resources with sales is very dependent on marketing.

5. **They usually have a high ratio of fixed costs to variable costs**. Manufacturing and trading businesses have a relatively high level of variable costs because of the need to purchase raw materials and finished goods and because of the employment of unskilled labour. Service industries usually require highly specialised staff even at relatively low skill levels. For example, your average factory laborer could not be put straight into portering at a hotel or cooking in a restaurant. In many cases, the service business mainly uses highly skilled staff. This means that very little of the labour is safely regarded as a variable cost. It is virtually all fixed cost.

This means that service businesses have break-even points that require the sale of a high level of services. There is very little latitude for personnel not to be fully employed in selling their time and expertise.

6. **There is not usually a standard product.** In some service businesses the products are just as standardised as they are in a factory. This is most obvious in the fast-food industry. However there is an argument for classing such businesses as manufacturers rather than services. In most of the service industries there is no standard product. A doctor may see twenty patients in a day, all with different symptoms and problems. A plumber may carry out a hundred tasks, all different. A computer consultant may work on several completely different computer applications in the space of a week. This has implications for the costing and pricing done in the business.

In recent years, because of the difficulties created by nonstandard products in costing and control, there have been several moves made to standardise services. Some of the more obvious attempts in this direction are in the travel industry where packaged tours standardise the service. Prescribed courses in tertiary education are another example. Standard service contracts issued by television service firms are also an attempt to standardise.

7. **Quantity measurement is difficult in service businesses.** In the manufacture of goods, we can easily measure the material inputs and the quantity of outputs that go into inventory. We can easily monitor the physical quantity of goods taken away by customers. Services cannot be measured in the same way. In a hospital it is possible to measure the number of patients treated and the number of bed/days of patient treatment, but you cannot measure the quantity of services provided. There is a pool of service providers who provide various combinations of services to the patients. Some patients may use up ten times as much

value in services as others. This often creates difficulties in setting some basis for the charges made. In a hospital the charge is based largely on time, which may only partly reflect the effort and cost of treating the patient. In nearly all cases in service businesses, charges are based on time, often with extra charges for certain inputs. However, this does not solve the problem entirely.

8. **Quality measurement is also difficult.** Defects in the quality of tangible goods are relatively easily and quickly detected. This is often not the case in service situations where judgment of the service may be more subjective. A legal firm may prepare a document which appears to be perfect. Then twenty years later a weakness or fault in a court case may cause major problems. A doctor may appear to cure a patient but symptoms may appear again several years later. Sometimes the 'cure' may cause problems not for the patient but for the patient's children who are damaged by the 'cure'. A computer program designed for a particular purpose may be shown to be inadequate only as the business user grows. So measurement of quality is very difficult and many users of services will take them at face value. This has implications for both user and provider.

9. **Many service businesses are very small**, operating from a single location. In small organisations, with a higher degree of personal contact, there is less need for sophisticated management control systems. However, even the smallest business needs a budget, cost analysis, performance measurement and controls. So if you go to work for a service business you still need knowledge about all of these things, no matter how small it is.

## Performance Measurement in Service Industries

Since service businesses are quite different in their structure and general characteristics, there are major differences in the way in which they operate. The goals of the organisation are different.

In a manufacturing business and in some service businesses such as the motel industry, the main criterion of performance is return on investment (ROI). In many service businesses the tangible assets used are relatively small in value and ROI is a totally inappropriate way to set goals. An electrician, for instance, may make a profit of $50 000 from assets of $4000.

The ROI is 1250 per cent, but it's not relevant anyway. To set a desired ROI as a target for performance in these circumstances is meaningless.

Clearly the skill of staff is the critical feature of the business and the assets are barely relevant to its goals. So goals must be set either on the basis of financial return per hour of service provided, or in terms of customer satisfaction.

The output of a service business can seldom be measured as units, liters, tonnes or kilograms. Revenue earned can be used as a measure of work done, but it measures only the quantity charged for, not the actual quantity of service inputs or the quality of the service provided. Because charges are usually related to time, output may be measured in hours of service provided. How do you measure the true value of the advice received from a doctor?

A doctor received an excited call from a woman:

'Doctor, doctor. My little boy just swallowed thirty aspirins. What can I do? What can I do?'

'Just kick him in the head and give him a headache - what else?'

That doctor's twenty dollars earned for giving the advice still becomes part of the output measurement.

The work of professionals tends to be non-repetitive, so planning of time and resources and setting of performance standards is difficult. Some professionals are reluctant to work to time constraints or to keep records of how time is spent. Research scientists, for instance, will often refuse to account for their time. You would strike tremendous resistance, and fairly so, if you told hospital doctors that costings indicated that they must see ten patients per hour. However, it is possible to develop production standards for any activity. Not surprisingly, it is in America where this has reached its heights. Some car rental companies have production standards for all activities along these lines.

1. No more than three customers shall wait in line without being attended to, at any one time, on more than two occasions in a day.

2. There shall be no more than one complaint per day of any unsatisfactory vehicle.

3. No telephone shall be allowed to ring more than twice before being answered.

Service-oriented companies must have service-oriented standards of performance.

## Everybody is a Marketer in a Service Industry

Often in service businesses there is no clear dividing line between marketing efforts and production efforts. This may be due to ethical standards or because of the nature of the contact between customer and service. Marketing is still required but it changes its nature to personal contact, speeches, articles in professional journals and in popular magazines, golf games, meetings of professional groups and so on.

- A doctor may be looking after the marketing angle in developing what is known as a 'good bedside manner'.
- The mere physical surroundings of a bank or lawyer's office may be part of the marketing technique.
- A clinical psychologist may advertise her abilities through appearances on radio or television.

- A corporate investment specialist may play golf in the right circles, which gives him contact with the right people.

The nature of these marketing techniques makes it almost impossible to allocate credit for the marketing effort to any particular individual.

## Pricing of Services

In companies selling goods the rate of return required on the assets used may underlie the pricing structure. This is not relevant with services, as we have seen. In practice, pricing is often fairly arbitrary, relying on traditional price structures not necessarily related to supply and demand. Accountants and lawyers have always charged more per hour than scientists who seem to be ranked low in status compared with their training. This may end one day.

There's a wonderful story about a vast team of scientists who built a huge electronic brain. It took twenty years and the monster was four stories high and a city block long. It had three million transistors and twenty thousand kilometers of memory tape. Its megabyte capacity was immeasurable. At last the team was ready; everything was humming smoothly. The world's top scientists sat down and discussed what should be the first question to ask the brain. After hours of deliberation, they settled on the most difficult question they could think of, 'Is there a God?'

A technician fed the question into the brain and suddenly the whole machine lit up, disks rotated and counters clicked and three words appeared on the giant screen.

'There is now!'

There are some service industries where methods used are similar to those used with goods. Pricing of airline fares, motel rooms and private school fees are examples of this approach.

## Use of Management Accounting Techniques

In recent years, management accounting has found much wider use in service industries. In general management accounting is used for four main purposes:

- inventory valuation
- cost control
- short-term planning; and
- product-profitability analysis.

Only the latter two are of great significance in service industries. Since inventories are seldom a significant asset, the distinction between product cost and period cost is not important. Virtually all costs are period costs as there is no tangible product. The only inventories are stocks of incidental materials, so inventory has little impact on profit calculation.

Service businesses must control costs, particularly administrative costs, but standard costing will seldom be used. Although some large accounting firms processing taxation returns do use a form of standard costing. Performance reports will still be prepared showing budgeted and actual revenue and costs. Variances will still be highlighted and closely investigated.

Much of short-term business planning relates to management of materials, direct labour and variable overheads. Service businesses do not usually have much connection with these.

## Service Firms and Break-Even Analysis

Usually little will be achieved by separating costs into fixed and variable, and often the assumption is made that all costs are fixed. However, this does not prevent the use of break-even analysis, which may be calculated on an hours-of-service basis rather than on unit output.

For example, suppose that Computer Services Pty Ltd predicts for the forthcoming year that fixed costs are $180,000, variable costs are no more than $5 per hour, and that the four employees will each do about 800 hours of consulting which will be charged out at $80 per hour. The first thing to do is to look at the break-even point to see whether the business is likely to be viable. The basic unit used will be the service hour.

$$\text{B/E point in service hours} = \frac{\text{Fixed costs}}{\text{Contribution margin per hour}}$$

The contribution margin per hour is the:

$$\text{Hourly fee} - \text{Variable costs per hour}$$

That is, in this case:

$$\$80 - 5 = \$75 \text{ per hour}$$

So,

$$\text{B/E point in service hours} = \frac{\$180\,000}{75}$$
$$= 2400 \text{ hours}$$

Since the business expects to sell about 3200 hours of service, we can see that it is a viable business. If only 75 per cent of the expected services are sold, the business will still break even.

We can also calculate the budgeted profit from this data. The expected 3200 hours is 800 hours above the break-even point of zero profit. Beyond that break-even point, all contribution margin becomes profit. So the profit should be:

$$800 \text{ hours} \times \$75 = \$60\,000$$

## Other Measures of Performance

In many service industries, other measures may be important in measuring performance such as bed-occupancy in hospitals, room-occupancy percentages in hotels, seat occupancy percentages in theatres and airlines, and percentage of available hours booked in consultancy services. Most industries have their own particular set of critical measures.

## Profitability Analysis of Services

All services provided can be described as products. Banks describe investment opportunities as products, packaged tours are referred to as products, insurance policies are insurance products. There is still an essential difference in the personal nature of services that makes them quite different from tangible products, but in using profitability analysis they can be treated like ordinary products. Profitability analysis can be used to help diagnose problems, to guide planning, and to analyse trends.

In order to diagnose problems, for example, products can be ranked in order of profitability, then some unprofitable products can be analysed in full detail and decisions made on the effects of discontinuing them.

A particular tour, back-packing in Iraq for instance, may not be selling up to expectations and the resources put into arranging it may be more profitably put into a tour of the great cricket grounds of England. Trends which give leads to new prospects can also be picked up from the nature of the most successful products. High-profit products might be expanded and new similar products introduced. Detailed analysis of individual products may be very valuable.

Changes in profitability can be analysed to aid in diagnosing potential problems. This can lead to a detailed review of all the service products offered, with the aim of seeing where most of the growth is occurring.

Profitability can also give a guide to pricing, indicating where prices could be cut if necessary to improve the competitive position. It may also indicate that some services offered are under-priced, but this must be considered in the light of competitive services and their prices.

Calculating the cost of providing a particular service is very difficult where the same inputs may assist in creating several types of service. The cost of a particular service will commonly be made up of the unique costs that go into that service, such as the salary costs of a particular employee and resources specific to that service; and an arbitrary assigned cost to cover general expenses.

Pricing may be based on a cost-plus formula which takes the result of this calculation and adds a set margin, say 20 per cent, or 50 per cent, or 200 per cent if that is what the market will bear.

To take an example, suppose that one of our employees costs us $25 per hour to employ with ancillary on-costs for holiday pay, annual leave loading, workers compensation and so on, of 25 per cent. The facilities used in providing the service cost $5 an hour in services and upkeep. In all we work 10 000 hours a year with unallocated costs of $80 000.

It is quite easy to work out the cost of providing an hour of service.

| | |
|---|---|
| Cost of employee ($25 + $6.25) | $31.25 per hour |
| Cost of facilities | 5.00 per hour |
| Assignment of general expenses | |
| $80 000 / 10 000 hours | 8.00 |
| COST OF PROVIDING SERVICE | $44.25 per hour |

If we found that this particular employee was earning fees for only 70 per cent of available hours, we could take that into consideration and adjust the costing so that it would cover the full cost of the employee.

Adjust for unused hours when 70 per cent occupied:

| | | |
|---|---|---|
| Cost of employee | $31.25 per hour | |
| $\frac{100}{70}$ × $31.25 = | | $44.64 |
| Add cost of facilities | | 5.00 |
| General expenses | | 8.00 |
| COST OF PROVIDING SERVICE | | $57.64 per hour |

If you were silly enough, you could add your 20 per cent mark-up to that and bill at that rate. Most wise service business people would first look around and see what the opposition is charging. If they are charging $100 an hour you could offer the service at $90 an hour knowing that you are doing very well. If the service is competitive in price and the market is there for it, you would soon fill the employee's appointment book and this will mean a drop in cost per hour for the service.

So services will become increasingly available and probably increasingly demanded as new areas of service open and old ones expand. People will always want to try new products and services, sometimes illogical. Some services are built on lack of logic.

Has it ever worried you, for instance, that people work night and day to buy labour-saving devices? And that people will pay someone else to do the mowing and gardening so that they've got time to pay to work out in a gymnasium?

# 16

## Out-Guessing the Competition: Planning and Strategy

Now that you're armed with all of the financial knowledge and a large bucket full of ideas, we will just take a quick look at some of the ways in which it can be used. To a certain extent it is a matter of not only what you do, but how you do it.

It was Mark Twain who said: 'All you need in this life is ignorance and confidence, and then Success is sure.' There is a certain amount of truth in that. Sometimes knowing a little too much can be inhibiting.

Scientific studies made on a school of fish in a tank have found that if you take one of the fish and carefully remove its brain, then put it back in the fish tank, it will become leader of the school.

Other studies made in the harsh realities of the business world indicate that plans, strategy and tactics are what it is all about. The American philosopher R. W. Emerson is reputed to have said that: 'If a man write a better book, preach a better sermon, or make a better mousetrap than his neighbour, though he build his house in the woods, the world will make a beaten path to his door.' There have been a million people and a million companies who have gone bankrupt waiting for them to find the woods, much less the house.

**In life, and in business, planning is essential.** All individuals and organisations plan. The types of plans developed may run into reams of computer paper or may be just an inkling in the back of someone's mind. They are all plans. The corporate plans developed by companies are amongst the most comprehensive of formal plans covering every aspect of the company. There is an Irish book on planning which says: 'You always get to where you plan. So if you don't plan to get there, you won't get to where you planned.'

## The Need to Plan

All organisations these days should be continually asking questions. Where are we going? How will we get there? What happens when we get there? If they don't, they will fail to reach their potential and may even get completely lost. There are three main reasons for planning:

- The first is that business conditions change so rapidly that corporate planning is necessary to anticipate future problems and identify opportunities.

- The second is that corporate planning provides employees with clear goals and directions to the future of the business.

- The third is that there is a tremendous amount of evidence that proves that businesses with a corporate plan are more effective than those without.

So planning is essential but one word of warning. **A plan must not become a straitjacket.** You must always keep a certain amount of flexibility.

## Corporate Planning

Corporate planning is the process which leads to the development of a corporate plan. It shapes and reveals the objectives of the firm, its purposes and goals. It produces the main policies and plans for achieving the goals, and defines the type of organisation the business hopes to become. So what is the difference between corporate planning, long-range planning, strategic planning, business policy, and strategic management?

The short answer is that there isn't any difference. The essentials of corporate planning are that:

- It looks to the future. Decisions made now have severe consequences for the future. Changing the future means making decisions now. Corporate planning can make sure that opportunities are grasped and pitfalls are avoided.

- It is a process which helps to decide in advance what should be done, when it should be done, and who should do it.

- It sets a philosophy which will be seen in everything that the business does, the attitudes of management, and the business environment.

- It will integrate short-term, medium-term, and long-term plans.

## What Is in the Corporate Plan?

The corporate plan is broader and more comprehensive than just financial planning marketing planning and budgeting but all of those plans will spring from it and be consistent with it. It is a fluid process which incorporates changes and trends as they occur. It does not make future decisions, it shows the way for current decisions which will create that future.

The contents of the corporate plan will differ according to the characteristics of the business. A company group will usually have an overall plan and separate plans for each subsidiary company. Some of these plans may not be formalised. Large companies sometimes have separate divisional plans. In the American giant, General Electric, each division is treated as a separate entity. Divisions are called SBUs (Strategic Business Units). Each SBU has its own strategic plan with these elements:

- a mission statement which sets out what kind of business it is in and what it is trying to achieve
- the key environmental assumptions about the external world, its opportunities and threats
- the key assumptions about competitors
- the list of external and internal constraints imposed on the division
- the desired future position, the SBU's objectives; * intermediate goals to be reached at specific times on the way to reaching objectives
- the strategy to be followed in achieving the objectives
- the program of development and investment required which is critical to the success of the strategy
- the required resources and where they will come from
- contingency plans which set out alternative strategies if something goes wrong and
- a financial flow statement setting out financial data which can be integrated with the existing financial controls.

## Who Does the Planning?

Most textbooks will tell you that the corporate plan should be 'the role and duty of the corporation's senior executive team'. Well who is that? It will depend on the company. The corporate plan requires a planning horizon of about ten years and a certain amount of initiative and inspiration. In some companies the Board of Directors will fit the bill. In most companies it won't. The last thing you want is for a bunch of crusty old corporate dinosaurs to be deciding the company's long-range future.

So, in many companies it will be the top operational management that does most of the corporate planning. Many of our fastest growing companies are lucky enough to be led by vigorous, progressive, aggressive individuals who take on the role of planning virtually single-handed. It must be said that many of these people use an approach euphemistically referred to as 'intuitive-anticipatory planning'. That is, the good old 'by guess and by God' method. It certainly works for them but the chances are that it won't work for the rest of us. What we require is formal corporate planning.

As a general rule specialist corporate planners or corporate planning teams are of limited benefit. All available evidence shows that such staff seldom have much input into the final plans. This is the job of the firm's top executives. Although accountants like to stick their oar into all of this, they should not play a major part, as the corporate plan is not a financial document. They may provide advice and information, as may lawyers, but neither accountants nor lawyers should be left to make the decisions.

## Corporate Objectives

We have said that corporate objectives are a critical part of the corporate plan. Corporate objectives are generally grouped into three categories:

### Basic Objectives

First there are basic objectives. These are the fundamental underlying objectives, including the product philosophy and mission philosophy, setting out what kind of business the company sees itself as being part of. These will include:

- financial and profitability objectives which set down parameters for the future financial position and anticipated profit levels.
- social objectives, such as broadening the employment of women, starting schemes for the employment of

handicapped persons, or trying to alleviate poverty in their area.

- psychological objectives that refer to influencing the attitudes of the public. Psychological objectives are important in industries like the tobacco industry where the product is controversial.

**Fulfilling objectives**

These are objectives that must be reached before the basic objectives can be fulfilled. They are usually designed to maintain or modify the company's market position as to placing of products and market share; its resources including materials, labour and capital; and its relationships with the various components of the environment inside and outside the firm. This may include the relationship with other businesses in the same group, competitors, governments, suppliers and distributors.

**Policies**

These are broad guidelines for the action to be taken in pursuit of the other objectives. They are general rules of action which are intended to ensure that the fulfilling objectives are achieved. Since each firm has its own unique set of fulfilling objectives, policies may also be quite different. However, all firms face similar issues and policies tend to be required that address certain issues. These might include:

1 Customer policy. How do we treat customers? Do we go soft on warranty claims? What sort of customer are we after?

2 Product policy. Do we make cheaper or quality products? Or both? What sort of products do we sell? What will we not sell?

3 Pricing policy. How do we set prices? Where do we see our positioning in the market? Up-market or down-market? Cost plus or what the market will bear?

4   Financial policy. Will we gear up with borrowings? Or are we conservative, financed by equity? How will we raise the capital required?

5   Personnel policy. Will we train our own, or poach skilled labour? How do we feel about ethnic minorities? What about women employees, what will we let them do?

6   Purchasing policy. Will we buy in or make it for ourselves? Will we import? Will we try to develop local sources of supply?

The corporate plan will concentrate on the basic objectives, the other two groups of objectives will be mainly addressed in subsidiary plans.

The leading American corporate planner, Jack Argenti says that the situation is really much simpler than all of this. He says that 'there is only one corporate objective that is always valid in all conceivable circumstances for all 'capitalist companies, namely, return on shareholders' capital.' This may be an important consideration, but I would suggest that it is not the full picture.

Most corporate planning is done with some vision of wider achievements than simple returns to shareholders. This is because the managers doing the planning will have their own sets of goals which are not necessarily consistent with those of the shareholders. Maybe it should not be like that, but I suspect that it is.

## The Position Audit

An integral part of the corporate plan is called the position audit. This is an appraisal of the current environment. Top management will keep an eye on what is happening in the market place and their industry to look out for opportunities and threats. They must also be influenced by the expectations of outsiders and insiders.

Outsiders include governments and the general public. Although economists still assume that businesses attempt to maximise short-term profits, a large business organisation cannot escape government, media and public scrutiny. It must, among other things, worry about pollution control, company image and social responsibility.

Insiders are mainly employees and shareholders. Individuals like to belong to companies that are 'industry leaders' or who produce the 'best product' or 'look after their employees'. These expectations must be considered in the planning process.

The size and nature of the business will largely determine another set of questions asked about corporate opportunities and weaknesses. Market size, product range and return on investment will all help in measuring those opportunities and weaknesses. These can be compared with other firms through analysis of their company reports. The company's own reports are analysed closely for signs of strengths and weaknesses. Product and product-line profitability, sales growth, return on investment, and residual income of divisions are all significant in making an assessment of strengths and weaknesses.

Implementing strategy requires that top management communicate the plan to the rest of management. The process also involves organising people and resources to reinforce the decisions made. Consistent policies will be required to back up the decisions. The parts of the plan must be co-ordinated so that they work together effectively. Once the corporate plan is in place there must be commitment throughout the firm to making it work.

Capital expenditure decisions and annual budgets must be consistent with the corporate plan. There is usually a tier arrangement of plans where the corporate plan is broken into divisional plans and one-year profit plans. The short-term plans must be consistent with long-term objectives. If they are not consistent, the whole planning exercise will be a waste of time. As we saw in chapter 7, budget planning will play a fundamental role in ensuring that short-term plans comply with the longer term plans.

Successful strategies can only be developed by taking into consideration the three main groups affected by strategies and influencing them at the same time:

- the company itself
- the customers and
- the competitors.

Strategies can be developed which are based primarily on any one of these groups.

## Company-Based Strategies

The main aim of company-based strategies is to build up the company's strengths in those areas which are crucial to success in its industry.

These key factors for success differ greatly from industry to industry.

- In most metal-refining industries, the key factor is high-quality sources of ore because low-quality ore is much more expensive to process and has much lower yields. An aluminium refiner which does not have high-quality bauxite sources will surely be uncompetitive.
- In the electronics industry, access to the latest technology is the key factor.
- In the copying machine industry, speed of service is the key factor as breakdowns are frequent.

So the business must be aware of what the key factors are in its industry and work on building them up as strengths.

Sometimes the company's strength may grow out of a structural situation. The Japanese firm, Casio, for instance, makes watches and calculators in competition with companies that are heavily involved in engineering and manufacture. Casio does very little of its own manufacturing. It mainly uses bought-in components, and assembles the product. This gives Casio much greater flexibility than its competitors because it has little invested in its production facilities. As a result the company competes by producing new products on a short product-life cycle. It produces a novelty product, then moves on to something else quickly. Its competitors are left floundering as their production facilities require that they be committed to a product for a couple of years.

The obvious way for competitors to combat this is to try to tie up the outside resources that Casio relies on, but they have not succeeded in doing this.

In a fragmented market the key factor is the distribution network. A good example is magazine distribution. Newsagents' shops are situated all over Australia, and most magazines are distributed through newsagents. Gordon and Gotch has for years dominated the distribution to newsagents. Its big strength is its distribution network, which enables it to increase its range of products supplied to newsagents, including stationery and books. It would be almost impossible for a competitor to get a toehold in this industry because the cost of setting up a competitive infrastructure is so great and there is probably not room for two companies in the industry.

Cost effectiveness is another area where firms can be more competitive. There are several ways in which firms can get more for their dollar, including minimising costs through budgeting and cost analysis; being more selective in the orders taken, products offered or services provided; and sharing costs across different product lines by introducing new lines compatible with existing company strengths. Some home-delivery pizza shops are now expanding into home-delivery spare ribs in order to share costs across different products.

## Customer-Based Strategies

In customer-based strategies the tendency these days is to segment the market and target a market segment with a particular product. In many cases the major segments become very competitive, and increasingly businesses seek unsatisified market niches for more specialised products. This trend can be clearly seen with magazines, books, motor vehicles, breakfast cereals, wines and vegetarian foods.

Markets can be segmented either by objective or customer coverage. If they are segmented by objective, the question is, 'How or why does the customer use this product?' Take soup for instance. Some people use it as a first course at dinner time, some as a snack, others as a warm-up lunch, others as a survival food. The way it is prepared, the ingredients, and the way it is eaten, will all differ according to the segment. The approach to marketing soup to each segment will be quite different.

If a market is segmented by customer coverage, the question is, 'How much of the market do we want to cover?' There always comes a point where marketing costs are higher than the additional revenue to be gained. This is why home-delivery pizza shops only deliver within a particular radius.

Sometimes a business can re-assess the segmentation, and create a strong competitive position by re-segmenting the market. At one stage the hot-water service industry was dominated by wood-chip heaters. Then gas water-heating was introduced. The segmentation was largely rural/urban because there were plenty of wood chips in the country and gas was obtainable only in the cities.

With the introduction of electric hot-water services, the urban market was split mainly on the basis of the age of the house. Nearly everyone wanted electricity because of its storage capacity. Then cheap natural gas led to the development of new mains-pressure storage gas hot-water services. Now the market has changed again because of the existence of a whole new market segment driven by environment-consciousness, and solar hot-water services are a growing trend.

Companies must always look for trends and the likelihood of new market segments. The 'greenie' market is not only fertile ground for solar hot-water services but for bush-covered housing blocks, country retreats and hobby farms; four-wheel-drive vehicles, hiking gear, tents, portable barbecues, sleeping bags and protective clothing; non-aerosol pressure packs; anything made from recycled waste; and battery-operated vehicles.

Customer-based strategies are at the foundation of all strategy. If a company loses sight of the real needs of its customers as they change over time, it will be vulnerable to attack from its competitors.

## Competitor-Based Strategies

Competitor-based strategies are the other main group. One significant area of strategy which arises from observing your competitors is product differentiation. The differences between your products and those of your competitors will be related to price, availability, cost, or status.

Too often in Australia we assume that price is the only effective weapon and allow our price structure to be dominated by those of our competitors. It is just as effective to have a product which is more easily obtainable than that of the competitor, which can be produced more cheaply or which has more user-status. Volvo cars don't sell in Australia because they are cheaper, they sell because of their high-status image. It is interesting that the Volvo car doesn't have the same level of status in its native Sweden. The image has been created by skillful marketing.

Image is one of the most powerful motivators in the market place and is often the result of more effort and resources being put into public relations and promotion. Where a leading product has an unassailable image position, competitors may try another tack. They may try new technology to switch the basis of competition. Japanese watch companies decimated the Swiss watch industry by using the new digital technology. The Swiss are fighting back by using a combination of price and new status with the 'Swatch'.

## Using Financial Information as a Competitive Tool

If you are able to analyse your competitors' cost structures using some of the techniques we have looked at, you may be able to exploit that to your company's advantage. For example, you could look at differences in the ratio of fixed cost to variable cost. If your company has a higher degree of fixed cost than your competitor, it is likely to be because the competitor buys in most components rather than making them. If times are hard, your competitor can cut prices more easily than you can because you are locked into high fixed costs which give you a high per unit cost. The smaller the market the bigger your losses. On the other hand, when the economy recovers, your competitor will face a bottleneck in getting supplies and your ready access to supplies from your own productive resources will enable you to seize a bigger share of the market.

Differences in size could also be examined. Larger companies will generally have higher fixed costs because of their greater investment in permanent resources. Smaller companies have higher variable cost proportions. So if you are a large company you should try to take advantage of the low variable-cost, high fixed-cost position and compete through price cutting, for instance. You have a bigger contribution margin per unit than the smaller firm and price cutting hurts them more than you as it will devastate their contribution margin.

For instance, if we had two firms, Large Ltd and Small Ltd, which compete in the same market, they may have completely different cost structures.

|  | Large Ltd | Small Ltd |
| --- | --- | --- |
| Turnover ($) | $10 million | $1 million |
| Fixed costs ($) | $2 million | $400 000 |
| Selling price per unit | $10 | $10 |
| Variable cost per unit | $2 | $5 |
| Contribution margin per unit | $8 | $5 |
| Budgeted sales (units) | 1 million | 100 000 |
| Budgeted profit | $6 million | $100 000 |
| Break-even point (units) | 250 000 | 80 000 |

As you can see, Large Ltd has a much greater margin of safety than Small Ltd. The obvious strategy is for Large Ltd to cut its price to, say, $7 per unit. Small Ltd has to cut prices to the same level to keep its market share because it has such a small safety margin. If it loses sales of 20 000 units, it starts to make a loss. At that price level Large Ltd is still making $5 per unit contribution margin. When Small Ltd cuts its price to $7 it is making only $2 per unit contribution margin and requires sales of 200 000 units just to break even. That appears to be well beyond its capacity.

Something else that may be worth analysing is differences in source of profit. Suppose there are two companies that sell copying machines. Super Copiers Ltd makes nearly all of its profit from servicing and very little from sales of new copiers. Dooper Copiers Ltd makes nearly all of its profit from sales of new equipment and very little from servicing. Dooper Copiers Ltd is very vulnerable because if Super Copiers Ltd engages in price cutting, it can't compete. The price could be lowered to a level which wipes out Dooper Copiers Ltd and it can't retaliate because it is too weak in service and most people want service from their original supplier if it is available.

So where does all of this leave us? What do the techniques in the rest of this book have to do with strategy? Everything!

The analysis of balance sheets and profit-and-loss statements can help you in finding the weaknesses and strengths of the competition. That is why they are so reluctant to disclose information in their reports.

Knowledge of how to calculate cost of capital can allow you to compare your cost structure with that of competitors. It can tell you their target profit figures.

You can do break-even calculations on products competitive with your own and develop strategies based on this information.

You can use your budget to calculate 'what-if' type situations so that you are ready to counter your competitors' strategies.

You can look for weaknesses in competitors' operating cycles and try to optimise your own to make you more competitive.

Your knowledge of cost centers, revenue centers, profit centers and investment centers can be applied to locating strengths and weaknesses in the competition.

Just about all of the techniques that you have looked at have this double purpose. They will help you play a more meaningful part in the day-to-day activities of your own firm and they can be applied to help you understand your competitors better. Two benefits for the price of one. There is always another angle, a better way to do things. Strategy is of critical importance.

The young man crept anxiously into the sales manager's office. He pulled nervously at his tie.

'Er, excuse me. You don't want to buy any life insurance do you?'

'No. Of course I don't.'

'I didn't think you would.' He headed hurriedly for the door. 'Oi wait a minute', the sales manager said. 'I've been training sales people all my life and you're about the worst I've ever seen. You'll never make any sales because you lack confidence in yourself. Chin up, man, be positive. I'll tell you what I'll do. Just to give you some confidence I'll take a $100 000 policy.'

The young man carefully filled out the proposal and the sales manager signed it.

'There you are, man. Bet that makes you feel better already. That's what you have to do, learn some tricks of the trade.'

The young man smiled. 'Thank you very much. You're absolutely right about the tricks of the trade', he said. 'The one I just used is especially for sales managers.'

So there you have it, an outline of the matters financial that may affect you as a manager. I hope that you have learned a few things from this book, but above all else that you have gained some confidence in dealing with accountants on their own territory. This should make you a more valuable manager and reward you accordingly. Good luck.